Law and the Social Sciences

✦

LAW *and the*
SOCIAL SCIENCES
in the Second Half Century

JULIUS STONE

UNIVERSITY OF MINNESOTA PRESS
Minneapolis

NORTH CENTRAL PUBLISHING COMPANY, ST. PAUL

Library of Congress Catalog Card Number: 65-12433

This book includes certain ideas and a number of passages which are also to be published in the author's *Social Dimensions of Law and Justice,* notably from Chapter 1, 1–6, and Chapter 14, 4–14, as well as ideas and passages from his *Legal System and Lawyers' Reasonings.* The latter work appeared after the Pattee Lectures were delivered in 1964 and the former work will appear in April 1966. The consent of the publishers (in the United States, Stanford University Press; in the United Kingdom, Stevens and Sons Ltd.; in Australia, Maitland Publications Pty. Ltd.) to the concurrent use here of the relevant passages is gratefully acknowledged.

PUBLISHED IN GREAT BRITAIN, INDIA, AND PAKISTAN BY THE OXFORD UNIVERSITY PRESS, LONDON, BOMBAY, AND KARACHI, AND IN CANADA BY THE COPP CLARK PUBLISHING CO. LIMITED, TORONTO

✛

TABLE OF CONTENTS

Law and the Social Sciences

WHERE LAW
AND SOCIAL SCIENCE STAND

I

IN THE FIRST HALF of the twentieth century the relations of the legal order with the wider social order became established beyond question as a central (perhaps the central) juristic and jurisprudential concern. Attention was increasingly directed to the effects of law upon the complex of human attitudes, behavior, organization, environment, skills, and powers involved in the maintenance of particular societies, or kinds of societies; and conversely on the effects of these upon the particular legal order. Insofar as a particular legal order is itself part of the social order in which it arises the interrelations involved include the influences of extralegal elements of the social order on the formation, operation, change, and disruption of the legal order, as well as the influences of the legal order (or particular parts, kinds and states of the legal order) on these extralegal elements. For the most part, though not exclusively, these inquiries have been pushed forward under the banner of sociological jurisprudence of which the greatest pioneers and champions were in this country Roscoe Pound, and on the European continent, Eugen Ehrlich and Hermann Kantorowicz. It is of the nature and scope of this established concern on the juristic side that I must first speak.

The subject-matter of such inquiries consists obviously of phenomena occurring in time and their relations with each other, and these may consist of phenomena of past societies as well as contemporary societies. Thus much of the work of the jurists known as the "Historical School" is better seen today as sociological jurisprudence applied to past societies and their legal systems, whether we think of the German historical school founded by Savigny at the beginning of the nineteenth century,[1] or of the English school founded by Maine half a century or more later. This work, especially that of Maine, joined forces with the work of the anthropologists; and it is remarkable how today, after decades in which Maine was a kind of whipping boy of anthropology, many of his basic insights often survive or revive with but minor qualifications even in the stream of contemporary anthropological knowledge.

Yet it has been for the contemporary world and its problems that the greatest energy and hope have been pinned on exploration of the interplay of legal and social change. In our age the central perplexities of Western legal orders are seen above all as manifesting the pressure upon the precepts and institutions of the law of the extralegal elements at play in social ordering. It seems almost self-evident today to see these perplexities in terms of the *de facto* claims pressing upon the legal *status quo* in title of individual life or in title of the social life (that is, of the social interdependence) of individuals. And we struggle to interpret even the most intractable conflicts of economic associations, whether of labor or of the giant corporations, including those of labor relations and antitrust law in these terms. Yet as a frame of reference for lawyers all this is so far from self-evident, that lawyers of earlier centuries were barely aware of it.

Earlier centuries of course, back into the earlier horizons of law and justice in the West, the great Judaeo-Christian, Greek, and Roman traditions, did concern themselves with theorizing and explaining law. But these traditions and their medieval and post-medieval successors were focused rather on one or both of two very different concerns. One of these concerns, which still survives into modern analytical jurisprudence, has its main focus on facilitating our vision of the logical coherence of the several propositions and parts of a legal order and on fixing the definitions of terms used and the presuppositions which will maximize such coherence. This kind of concern tends to identify "law" and "a legal order" only with those elements which are statable in the form of legal propositions. By contrast with this, sociological jurisprudence, and any study which seeks to bring social science knowledge to serve legal problems, address themselves to the influences of social, economic, psychological and other non-legal factors on the process of change in the concrete content of legal propositions. And they also attend to those parts of the legal order which, though not consisting of legal propositions, have a similar influence on these — for example, the technique and traditional ideals and the professional idiosyncrasies of lawyers. For all these are *facts* of the legal order, the relation of which to the facts of the more general social context it is the task of this discipline to examine.

The other main concern of earlier centuries and millennia in relation to law, itself among the oldest human concerns of any kind, has been to understand what justice is, to establish what justice requires that we ought to do and its particular bearing on law. It is clear that as a body of knowledge this is not identical with knowledge about the relations of law and society. The fact that men of a given society at a given time hold particular ideals of justice is in itself a part of the social facts to which the study of law and society is concerned to relate the legal order. And while it is true that the study of theories of justice is also concerned with such ideals, the standpoint is sharply different. The study of law in its social interrelations is concerned with the actual effects in the legal order of *the fact that such ideals are held,* and the effects of the legal order on such ideals as held. It is not concerned in principle, as is the study of theories of justice, with the question whether the ideals are valid, invalid, demonstrable or undemonstrable, useful or useless or indeterminate. The former is a descriptive activity; the latter is a normative or "evaluative" one. The one tries to describe what "is," or "goes on," the other what "ought to be" or "ought to go on."

This apparently clear distinction was overlaid in the last generation by two confusing factors. One was the tangled polemics between the main line of sociological juristic thought of Roscoe Pound, and the Neo-Realist demand of the late Karl Llewellyn for "the divorce of the Is and the Ought." The other was the fact that pragmatist theories of justice such as that of Pound himself purport to offer a method of measuring social facts *as a theory of justice*; Pound's own theory of justice has had to be ferreted out from the nooks and crannies, and the often concealed assumptions, of his sociological writings.

I have spoken thus far in terms of the interplay of law and other social phenomena. When we direct ourselves to the relations of law and "social science," that is, to the relations between the respective bodies of knowledge, rather than the subject-matters of these, we have to acknowledge additional complexities. The knowledge of this subject-matter is as yet still distributed over numerous social sciences, and the question whether these can be "unified" in some way or whether there is some master discipline such as sociology or anthropology transcending their plurality, has long been a *casus belli* among social scientists. It would be foolish for the jurist, who needs mutual aid pacts with all who bear the extralegal knowledge which he seeks, to join in these conflicts. In his study of law and society he must garner knowledge where knowledge is to be found, and must therefore call on all the mobile and expanding social sciences, including among the more traditional subjects, anthropology, economics, geography, psychology, and social medicine, and those concerned with social, ethical, and political institutions; and among the more modern subjects demography, social statistics, social psychology, and sociology.

He is concerned to bring such accumulated bodies of knowledge to bear, so far as they are relevant, upon legal problems, and to do so, as we have said, for both past and present legal orders. Moreover it is also among his tasks to bring the resulting findings concerning law and other social phenomena onto as general a level of statement as these will tolerate. Jurisprudential scholarship, indeed, has its own internecine strife as to whether there should not be a special "social science of law" or "sociology of law" consisting of general principles, as invariant as those of the natural sciences, concerning law as a social phenomenon. I shall have some remarks to make in due course concerning this; our present point holds in any case. A part of the tasks for aid in which the study of law must resort to the social sciences addresses itself on as general a level as possible to the social, economic, and psychological factors operative in legal stability and change. It must examine in the light of the facts the various theories of the non-autonomous nature of the law, for instance the Marxist-Soviet theory of the "withering away" of the State and law, and certain institutionalist theories. It must say what the state of knowledge permits concerning the relation of law to men's social-psychological interactions in their attitudes to problems of value raised by actual social and economic conditions. And there are related tasks concerning the relation of law to the power process in society, in its enormously varied aspects and degrees, all turning upon social-psychological interactions of varying complexity. The roles of the judge, administrator, and other functionaries in legal ordering cry out for reappraisal and perhaps even restructuring, by a union of juristic resources with those of the social sciences. And, perhaps above all, the jurist needs the social sciences for understanding how other social controls in modern democracy are related to law, what are the implications of this under given conditions of the extension of social control through law, especially for the participation of citizens and responsibility of rulers. For on this understanding, and our ability to guide our polities accordingly, the survival of the proudest achievements of free government may well now depend.[2]

II

HAVING thus drawn attention to the long-established juristic concern with the social relations of law, it is important that I now draw attention to the earlier streams of thought which preceded and contributed to this concern.

It is clear that it was fed by two distinct intellectual streams. From the juristic side the so-called historical jurisprudence, especially as fruitfully criticized by anthropology, moved out from study of the law itself to its social interrelations; while modern sociology, and particular social sciences such as anthropology, invaded the juristic field to try to explain law as one element of the social complex.

"Historical jurisprudence" provided sociological jurisprudence with the false colors, and the transient but effective password of the "*Volksgeist.*" [3] It introduced internal correctives to juristic logicism and abstract speculation as to justice,[4] which would not perhaps have been acceptable from early sociology flying its true colors under the command (as it were) of sociological "outsiders." Both on its German side, led by Savigny, and on its English side, led by Maine, the historical school drove home two important truths. First, it showed that law was intimately related to the social context, thus making juristically respectable and even commonplace what was philosophically and politically commonplace after Montesquieu. Further, these jurists propounded before Darwin a crude theory of evolution in the social field; in this crude sense the idea of evolution was already in juristic currency before it entered that of biology and early sociology. Second, these jurists challenged the competence of mere logical analysis as well as of a priori speculations as to justice. For by its nature the historical view directed attention to social facts intractable in such terms, against which indeed (in the last resort) juristic speculation might have to be tested. Historical jurisprudence thus not only led the jurists towards the promised land; it also reduced the main forts of its existing occupants. It played the role of Moses and, in part at least, of Joshua as well. But it was not to be under its own banner, but under that of sociological jurisprudence, that the promised land was to be conquered and occupied. In Saleilles' vivid words, "the historical school . . . remained as if glued to the spot, incapable of using the instrument of evolution and practice which it has just proclaimed." He blamed for this the fatalism which "could merely wait, register and observe," and which declined to face the challenge of "creative legislation and interpretation."[5] It is perhaps in the work of Willard Hurst of Wisconsin on law and economic growth that we should see the ablest contemporary attempt to transcend these limitations of the traditional historical jurisprudence.[6]

The search for fuller understanding of social life is of course far older than what in the last century or so has been dubbed sociology; and it is not necessary for me here, as some have done, to seek to fix its beginnings, whether at Confucius, or Plato, or some other point.[7] Montesquieu in the eighteenth century is an early enough point of modern departure, both in his indirect influence on certain great legal thinkers, like Beccaria and Bentham,[8] and in his direct impact on social and political thinking generally. The central thesis of the *Lettres Persanes* and of *L'Esprit des Lois*, that human laws and justice are the resultant of numerous factors such as the local manners and customs and physical environment, implied that human laws as social phenomena can be understood only by postulating the operation of cause and effect in the social field.[9] It challenged the current natural-law assumption that ideal rules of law were constant from age to age and from people to people, and could be discovered by contemplation of man's ideal nature;[10] and it laid the basis simultaneously of sociology in general and of sociological jurisprudence in particular.[11] It was only after this basis was laid that the juristic and sociological approaches separated out for a time until the *rapprochement* of the present century.[12]

One major stage of development after Montesquieu and his followers is usually seen in the influence of scientific analogies in sociological writing. The high point of this nineteenth-century trend is associated with the name of another classical French scholar, the leader of modern positivism, Auguste Comte, who lived through the first half of the nineteenth century, and whose *Système de Philosophie Positive ou Traité de Sociologie* was published 1852–54;[13] though eighteenth-century origins in the analogy of Newtonian physics have also been suggested.[14] The influence of the mathematical model upon Comte's sociology is undoubted. Comte was himself a teacher of mathematics and the era in which he lived was marked by obvious triumphs of the mathematical and physical sciences generally in bringing to light the structure and development of the physical universe. He saw his own times as the beginning of an era in which mankind, after successive failures to explain the world by theology and magic, and by metaphysical postulates about the "essence" of things, was to accept the positivist view. The facts of society, like those of the physical universe, were to be explained not by introducing a *deus ex machina* into the plot, but by relating them to each other by resort to hypotheses and their verification, and thus arriving at social laws comparable to the laws of physics and chemistry.

It is now well recognized that mechanical models are hazardous for social science, though in more sophisticated and less assertive but still hazardous refinements they may still underlie explicit assumptions or unspoken aspirations of many social scientists. Certainly in its Comtian form it was an inadequate frame for dealing with psychological (including group psychological) facts (the modern science of psychology was, after all, still in the future). Linked with this was its overconfident assertion of inexorable social trends, its overhaste to draw "laws" from data still obviously inadequate at that stage, and its tendency to confuse the discovery of "laws" explaining social phenomena with the justification of these phenomena.[15]

Charles Darwin's *Origin of Species by Means of Natural Selection, or the Preservation of Favoured Races in the Struggle for Life* broke on the world in 1859. How much of the credit of originality for this thesis has been unduly given to Darwin, rather than to his predecessors [16] and contemporaries,[17] has been brought into some doubt.[18] It may be that the idea of evolutionism by survival of the fittest in the social field owes more to Spencer than to Darwin, and that Darwin's own ideas did not go further than natural selection from accidental (non-purposive) variations. Even then, however, it was mainly as attributed to Darwin's *Origin of Species* that social evolutionism went into the stream of social thought, for instance through William James, W. G. Sumner, and John Dewey.[19] Biological interpretations sometimes took as the developing organism a particular people, yielding studies in the growth of institutions of an ethnological or demographic type; sometimes they sought to explain the dominance or disappearance of ideas [20] or classes [21] or peoples,[22] in the history of legal and other institutions, by the biological principles of the struggle for survival. In one form or another evolutionism, like many major ideas, burst the scientific compartment in which it arose; and the signs of its juristic influence have been legion.[23]

The early criticisms of social evolutionism, apart from those by bible fundamentalists, were mainly in terms of competing notions of evolutionism, rather than the modern type of questioning whether mental and moral growth are necessarily subjected to the laws of physico-biological growth. A notable pioneer of the later approach was Samuel Butler who in his *Erewhon* in 1872 not only saw clearly the emergence of both the Spencerian and Darwinian versions in earlier thought, but also pointed to the key role of an organism's interests or purposes and therefore of its own efforts, in originating the variations which in turn characterize the various species.[24]

Historically, however, the wane of the fatalistic evolutionism in the streams of sociological and juristic thought came rather from the growing interest in psychology. Five chief manifestations of this influence succeeded each other as the century ended and the new century opened: (1) the interest in group will and group psychology as actual phenomena distinct from those of the individuals of the group, traceable to the juristic work of Otto von Gierke; [25] (2) the theory of dynamic psychic drives as the causes of social phenomena and the call to use these drives in positive social action, traceable to the sociological work of Lester Ward; [26] (3) the theory of imitation as a primary psychic phenomenon contributing to the growth of law, traceable to the work of Gabriel Tarde.[27]

(Gierke, then, drew attention to the actuality, or as it is termed, "reality" of group will and attitudes; Ward proclaimed the possibility and necessity for a dynamic purposive use of such psychological phenomena in social planning; and Tarde offered a hypothesis, since proved over-simple,[28] of how these phenomena came about and how stability in group behavior arises—the psychological "law of imitation.") To these three influences there must certainly be added today at least two others: [29] (4) the theory of individual psychic activity on the unconscious level as an explanation of behavior irrational on the level of consciousness, traceable to the work of Sigmund Freud; and (5) the theory of the non-rational and irrational in social life in which the work of Vilfredo Pareto and Max Weber was pioneering, but which Emile Durkheim and others anticipated in important respects.[30]

Emile Durkheim,[31] followed in this respect by Léon Duguit, developed the inquiry into the correspondence between differences in social structure and differences in the law arising from those structures. He suggested that these correspondences should be traced to the kind of cohesive force, of "solidarity," by which a society is held together. Sociology thus by an independent route arrived at some of the central problems already raised from a narrower juristic viewpoint by Savigny and Maine — the relation between characteristics of a functioning social unit and the characteristics of its law.[32] The functionalism of Durkheim centered on the mutuality of support and adaptation between institutions in a given society, and the transmission of changes in one institution gradually to the rest (of which Duguit gave an over-rigid juristic version) became a main continuing theme of modern social science. And it drew ancillary support from the biological concept of *homeostasis*.[33]

Into this *rapprochement* of juristic and sociological preoccupations in the last quarter of the century, there also emerged economics-centered lines of thought proceeding from Marx and Engels and their followers, including not merely socialist jurists like Karl Renner, but important independent thinkers like Max Weber.

When the oversimplifications of Marxism are discounted, its insistence on the complex interdependence of the legal, ethical, economic, and psychological inquiries remained (and still remains) of capital importance.[34] And the thesis of the sociologist E. A. Ross's *Social Control* [35] placed the classical juristic question of the relation of law and morals into the context of a general theory of the functional kinship of a wider diversity of "means of social control," including religion, custom, current morality, and law. He identified law as merely "the most specialised and highly finished" of these means of social control.[36]

The end of the century, indeed, introduced a period of reciprocal stocktaking by the sociological explorers of law, and the juristic explorers of sociology. Saleilles (as we have seen) was reproaching historical jurisprudence for its futility and fatalism; and von Jhering's dynamic but often superficial generalizations also came under attack from the social scientists. Léon Duguit and Maurice Hauriou [37] were transplanting into juristic thought some main ideas of Durkheim. Eugen Ehrlich's juristic hypothesis that the center of gravity of legal development lies, not in legislation or juristic science or judicial decision, but in society itself, ran parallel to the anthropological view of law as a body of obligations kept in force by specific mechanisms of reciprocity and publicity deep within the structure of society.[38] With Ehrlich's *Beiträge zur Theorie der Rechtsquellen* in 1902, his *Soziologie und Jurisprudenz* in 1906, and his *Grundlegung der Soziologie des Rechts* in 1913; [39] with Hermann Kantorowicz's *Der Kampf um die Rechtswissenschaft* [40] in 1906, and his *Rechtswissenschaft und Soziologie* in 1911, the sociological and juristic lines of inquiry begin to flow in a single stream in Germany. With Roscoe Pound's famous articles on "The Scope and Purpose of Sociological Jurisprudence" in 1911,[41] the same process was well begun in the English-speaking world. If we are not cynically hypercritical or naively impatient and Utopian we have to acknowledge that mutual consultation and support, not only among the social sciences generally, but between them and jurisprudential inquiries, have steadily grown since that time. This is so apparent over so many areas that we think it fruitless to debate how far it falls short of the stage of "unification" of sociological approaches which Pound believed to have begun half a century ago.[42]

III

IN THE LIGHT OF this background I hope that it will not be thought jurisprudentially chauvinist to observe that "the revolt against formalism," by which Morton White in 1949 characterized the trends of the modern social sciences,[43] matured earlier in jurisprudence than it did in the social sciences. The reaction of Savigny against eighteenth-century natural law, of Jhering's social utilitarianism against the logicism of the Pandectists, and of Maine and the anthropologists and the early sociological jurists against merely technical professional preoccupation with law, all merged into a broad juristic anti-formalism which is still running its course. In the social sciences the revolt recoiled from excessive reliance on logic, abstraction, deduction, and the analogies of mathematics and mechanics.[44] It tended to shift the focus of attention first on to history, and the supposed organic process of cultural growth, and then broadly to the materials bearing upon the concerns of each social science which can be culled from the rest.

This later stage will be misunderstood and seem to be an activity of the blind leading the blind unless it is recognized that what lies behind it is an acknowledgment that the very distinctions between the subject-matters of the respective social sciences rest on abstractions with which nothing really corresponds in the sensually perceived world. When it is wittily said that social scientists have been summoned to unite by the call that "they have nothing to lose but their deductive chains," [45] this bears also the meaning that social scientists of each branch should try to transcend the very abstractions which base their own subject. Finally, of course, it also means abandonment of the assumption of the distinct identity of the scientist's own branch, for this is implicit in the recognition that all the social sciences finally have one common subject-matter. Some of the outstanding contemporary studies in social science, as we shall see, cannot be associated with particular social sciences, nor even with philosophy, but seem to address themselves simultaneously to all of these.

The strains of thought leading to the present position have multiple and varied texture. In the United States Morton White has detected mainly five.[46] One is the pragmatism and instrumentalism of the late John Dewey which holds that ideas are plans of action, and not mirrors of reality; that dualisms of all kinds are fatal; that "creative intelligence" is the best way to solve problems; and that philosophy ought to free itself from metaphysics and devote itself to social engineering.[47] A second is Thorstein Veblen's institutionalism, insisting upon the importance of studying empirically the connections between economic institutions and other aspects of culture. It rejected classical political economy as abstract and (while avoiding the Marxist interpretation of history) offered instead a programmatic theory of economic development in terms of the fundamental institutions of the engineers and the price system.[48] A third, of juristic as well as general interest, was the movement which came to be called "realism," and is traced to Oliver Wendell Holmes, Jr., rejecting the view that law is an abstract entity pre-existing and waiting to be found by a judge, and asserting, on the contrary that it is, in great measure, *made* by the judge.[49]

Fourth was the preoccupation, brought into the center of the stage by the historian Charles Beard, with the underlying economic forces which are thought to have determined the history of civilization, and continue to control the directions and acceleration of social life.[50] Linked finally with these influences, and (like all of them) having importance well beyond the American scene, was the changed view of history as no mere chronicle of the past, much less of mere kings and battles, but as a means of understanding the present and guiding the future of civilization.[51]

No thought, indeed, could be free at this stage from the broad movements of nineteenth-century European thought. These included above all the assertion of the possibility of onward movement, of progress, which underlay both the reviving and revising of history wrought by nineteenth-century romanticism; the Spencerian-Darwinian doctrines of evolution and survival of the fittest; the humanitarian drives inherited from the French rationalists and fed by the French and American revolutions; the rise of political pluralism as an ideal of social and political philosophy; the new approach to philosophy and knowledge emergent from the Newtonian model of natural science and the materialist interpretation of history from the formidable pens of Marx and Engels.

It is easy with hindsight to recognize that the great intellectual ferment proceeding against this background was inadequate to meet the problems which emerged from it. These included the problems of what is meant by "objectivity" in history, and how far it represents a real norm,[52] and above all whether, if metaphysics is to be dispensed with, it is possible through empirical methods to approach at all the central issues of the relation between social science and moral values.[53] On this matter, the giants of the antiformalist period stopped short with assertions of faith in terms of emphatic "Can't helps," or with a shrugging "Give it up," or vain struggles to find some way through between personal faith and amoralism. And we can now see, in White's words, why the revolt against formalism was "speedily followed by a reign of terror in which precision, logic and analytical method became suspect." [54] At any rate, neither social science nor sociological jurisprudence could rest easy at such a point. Even in the most pragmatic enterprise of physical engineering, let alone social engineering, aspiration and program cannot be dispensed with; for "only after we know the kind of bridge we want can we start building it. We may modify our original plans in the light of further discoveries and snags, but there must be hypotheses to begin with which will bend to meet the facts." [55]

In jurisprudential thought these deep difficulties, as we shall see, emerged with particular sharpness. The fact that lawyers by training and by the very nature of their subject-matter are committed to the idea of obligation and a belief in its reality, increased the sharpness; but it also limited, at any rate in the Western democracies, the terror of aimless anarchy which went with the more general anti-formalist revolt.

IV

EVEN IN 1946 the present author was concerned to set limits to the iconoclastic anarchy of this revolt in the juristic sphere, especially when this proceeded from enthusiastic haste. We rejected the view that the social movements of the period, including the intellectual movements, were all a direct outcome of technical and economical developments, whether this were understood in the rigid Marxist or in some more flexible versions. While conscious of the dangers involved, we refused to accept the grim view that these developments must lead inevitably to social and political disintegration. We were concerned, indeed, rather to bring to general attention those implications of the anti-formalist revolt which indicated that new kinds of social action might be available capable of preserving what was precious in the Western democratic inheritance. Those who share this kind of faith will be encouraged by many aspects of the epoch-making generation that has intervened to which I wish to refer at the close of this first essay.

I refer not merely to the remarkable physical survival and revival of the main Western democratic polities, and with this of the possibility of further extension of the benefits of their tradition to scores of newly independent states. I refer also more particularly to the revolution that is already an accomplished fact in the recognition of the human rights of industrial labor. And I refer no less to the growing recognition that technological trends (for instance towards automation) must be matched by farseeing social action in the realms of education and leisure (as well as in work itself), to prevent individuals from falling as casualties in man's battle with nature. In the more traditional areas of social life, despite momentary reverses and continuing pockets of intractability where external security is thought to be involved, the generation since 1945 has seen a resounding victory for civil and political liberties against odds which often seemed quite overwhelming. It has also seen, even under the inhuman shadow of nuclear weapons, the steady continuance of humanitarian concern with the backward, the handicapped, the unprivileged, and the oppressed, whether in the national or the international arenas. The need to confront problems of health, poverty, insecurity, and ugliness, with the only kind of action to which they will yield at all, namely that of collective thought, decision, and action, has established itself against what seemed like implacable political and social dogma, and immovable vested interest.

We add one further ground for optimism, without seeking to exhaust the matter. For various reasons already adverted to jurists have come to recognize that the evaluating activities of the study of justice must go along with the descriptive activities of sociological jurisprudence. And awareness has become sharper in the social sciences generally that questions of policy and justice still have to be settled after social science has done all it can, so that even the more practical disciplines like economics must somehow attend to and sometimes even wait on directives of policy and justice. Remarkable work like that of Gunnar Myrdal and J. K. Galbraith [56] has shown how often there lie behind the ostensibly empirical certainties of supply and demand, and their interrelations, conflicting versions of the good life and of consequential social policies, for which diverse economic theories are consciously (or by unconscious default) partisan.

Much work of this kind raises over the whole field of the social sciences a main question with which we were deeply concerned in 1946 for the legal area.[57] This was whether much of the drive to empirical inquiry concerning law and society would not sterilize itself unless it admitted to its side as both legitimate and necessary the concern with ethical judgment, and in particular with men's theories of justice. Fact-gathering, and even "scientific" generalization about facts gathered, we insisted, could not give more than a foundation for the central questions of the democratic legal order. These central questions were concerned with what *should be done* about the facts; they were questions of ethics, social policy, and justice. And whether or not these could be handled metaphysically we were at least clear that they could not be handled empirically.[58]

On such matters, therefore, the present writer insisted, and continues to insist, that the rebels against formalism cannot presume to plan from any scientific scratch, as if no guiding line or useful lead whatsoever need be drawn from the experience and learning of the pre-social-science age. In this insistence we drew comfort not only from juristic predecessors of the generation just past, but from notable stirrings among the younger generation of social scientists themselves. Talcott Parsons' *Structure of Social Action* had then already recently foreshadowed a broad approach to social knowledge which would respect the difference between facts and values, and yet set a place for each; and his later work, notably *The Social System,* has continued this impetus. The admirable program on "Social Values and Public Policy" in the political science department of the University of Pennsylvania inaugurated in 1960 has approached this whole complex of problems from an even wider and no less basic standpoint which holds great promise of orderly development.[59]

The great difficulty still plagues us of achieving this avoidance of amoralism without falling back into the mere theological or natural law absolutes. The great political, economic, and social issues of our times, as White has well said, "are not likely to be settled by an appeal to a theological dogma which demands a faith that is not shared by all honest and intelligent participants in the debate." Empirical social inquiry must be sophisticated enough to recognize the limits of its own competence; but its competence within its proper limits should also not be denied. We deny it when by some variant of the doctrine of "original sin" we deny man's capacity to recognize or create, and in any case to respect, ideal norms to which he should conform. We also deny it if we insist that somehow these ideal norms are given to man by a transcending order of natural law, not subject to his own powers of cognition and to his own reasoning from what is cognized. The one plunges men into impotence by overworking the truism that man is not God; the other does so by overworking the truism that man has an inescapable and unalterable "nature." Both, if we took them literally, would oust any serious competence of law and the social sciences. It is clear that the aid which the social sciences can give in our perplexities is neither quickly identified, nor facilely exploited, and the changing world steadily adds new perplexities to our lot. The temptation in these circumstances to escape into some kind of *iusnaturalism*, or some related doctrine of moral inevitability, is correspondingly great.[60] In the study of law and society we need to resist this temptation.[61]

The difficulty of thus steering between Scylla and Charybdis is increased by the hazards arising from other less well recognized but no less treacherous shoals and rocks. One of these rises up from our very successes in some fields of social science in the construction of over-all systematic theory, of which perhaps the Parsonian elaboration of "the social system" is itself an example. We have observed on the important advantages of this drive for over-all cognition of the subject-matter of a discipline, and the identification of key points within it, and on the infection of juristic thought with related tendencies. Yet we must also draw attention to the dangers of appropriating intellectual resources too exclusively in this direction. For, especially with subject-matters like the law (and in this regard government, psychiatry, and economics might equally be mentioned) which require daily action, and therefore daily choices, systematic theory can rarely be of aid save for the long run. For this long run, *present* decision-making cannot usually wait. There remains, therefore, an imperative need, in terms of the social relevance of knowledge, for substantial intellectual resources to remain *engagés* with the *ad hoc* problems thrown up by contemporary society, so that there may be adequate provisional conceptualization and the intelligent search for practical adjustments in these segmental areas also. We shall elaborate this point in the second essay, and shall there point out that this desideratum has importance not merely for practical action, but also for the necessary checking of *systematic* theorizing by the inflow of empirical data not handpicked for this purpose.

V

LET ME now conclude this opening essay by returning for a few moments from the wider relations of social science and the problem of value-choices among social policies, to a microcosm of this same problem which has already engaged lawyers and legal thinkers for about a century. For it is already as long as that since lawyers first began, under the slogan "A Ministry of Justice," debating the establishment of some branch of government which should concern itself, not merely with the ongoing administration of the law, but with constant reassessment of its adequacy for the time and place, the pinpointing of the failures of justice and social policy, and the prescription of remedies.[62]

It is also nearly half a century since Pound's call for the establishment of Ministries of Justice in common-law countries placed these imperative legal needs in terms of a demand for greater use in their fulfillment of the data of social sciences. He called for a constructive lawyership guided by what Holmes symbolized in "the man of statistics and the master of economics." [63] Since then three things have happened. One is that (for whatever reasons) it has become clear that common-law countries have not and are not likely to centralize the above tasks in comprehensive "Ministries of Justice." Another is that various parts of these tasks have nevertheless been allocated piecemeal, but often effectively, among diverse old or newer institutions. Legislative research bureaus and legislative councils, law school legislative research services and law revision commissions have grown up, as well they may in view of the accumulating mountain of 931 volumes of American statute law, to which legislators added in 1952–53 another 29,938 statutes. Judges have resorted to their rule-making power and organized themselves in Judicial Councils, and have begun to be served by "Institutes of Judicial Administration." Expert agencies, advisory and executive, have become an ever-proliferating part of modern legislative and executive, government. To the central government of the United Kingdom alone not fewer than 850 such agencies were attached in 1958, of which two thirds were specialized, mostly in social science; and these figures did not include merely ephemeral or *ad hoc* bodies. Various kinds of offices, like that of *Ombudsman* or parliamentary commissioner, have arisen for channeling and investigating criticisms of legal processes. Efforts have begun under United States federal auspices to establish the regular "Administrative Conference" as a channel of research, mutual consultation, and progressive development for the proliferating multitude of administrative agencies. Third, and this is what here concerns us, it has become clear that many of the steadily recurring tasks involved in ministering to justice involve far-ranging non-legal expertises and complexities still often beyond the reach of the personnel in the time available for handling them.

This last truth has gradually led to a certain change in approach by more thoughtful students of law reform. Hessel Yntema called, as early as 1934, for "institutes of legal research" for the tasks of reform, to be wholly devoted to "a fundamental and persistent examination of the administration of justice." [64] As the mid-century approached, not only Pound, but the deeply dedicated and experienced Arthur T. Vanderbilt [65] had secured some recognition by the profession that, "vast and complex" as modern law has become, it can only stay "vital in content, efficient in operation and accurate in aim" by borrowing truths "from the political, social and economic sciences," and "from philosophy." [66] Such views have converged in present tendencies to make the promotion of legal research a central objective, and to strengthen and widen it, not only by the provision of funds, but by associating with work in the law schools the efforts of experienced lawyers and judges, and of specialists in the relevant social sciences.

The emergent drive is for the "law center" as a vital ancillary, perhaps even a power house, for various institutions, public and private, active in legal reform.[67] Besides more long-term inquiries, such centers might take up specific aspects of the law in action in their full contexts. Among well-known examples are New York University's Institute of Judicial Administration, or Columbia's Project for More Effective Justice, or Harvard's Civil Liberties Research Bureau or the Law and Society Center at the University of California at Berkeley.[68] Vanderbilt's later conclusions placed much hope (we believe correctly) in the possibility of securing an effective flow of relevant data, arising from constant and wide-ranging research activity from such Law Centers to the organs (such as judicial councils, legislative councils and drafting offices, law reform committees, and offices of administrative procedure) directly concerned with oversight and reform.

Even in the United States this is still a limited movement. Yet British countries, too, officially recognized in the 'thirties the needed role of legal research. An Institute of Advanced Legal Studies was then established in London, as well as (in the 'forties) an Institute of Criminal Science at Cambridge.[69] Initiatives for the growth of Legal Centers, we may add, can be of varied origin. The remarkable achievement of the Bar Association of the City of New York, working with full-time personnel, shows that the core activity may thrive even away from universities and law schools.[70] Valuable initiatives have also come from foundations,[71] and an American Bar Foundation has for some time been preparing to enter the research area.

The translation into these modern and varied terms of the tasks of ministering to the ongoing needs of law and justice should not conceal the real proportions of what is required, and the great costs and dedication of personnel involved. However we institutionalize their performance, it will not reach an adequate level unless governments make available most of the resources required. At the same time, three considerations may strengthen the will to go forward. One is that the material and personnel resources committed would still be trivial compared with what we pour as a matter of course into research in natural science and technology. A second is that "while civilisation has survived in bygone eras without science, there never has been a civilisation which has survived without a system of law adapted to its peculiar needs." [72] A third is that unless we make progress here, even the greatest faith and pride in the common law will not assure its viability in the challengingly ominous conditions of our age.

Finally, we need to observe that while past champions of legal research in this context have mostly envisaged the task in terms of projects on *ad hoc* problems, this aspect may well become only a part (though an important part) of what is required. For as to some of the major problems of the legal order now looming, both the social sciences and the legal inquiries for which these serve as pre-ordinated bodies of knowledge, will increasingly have to seek understanding of the whole working order of relations so as to identify key points for adjustment in it, rather than particular trouble spots for merely *ad hoc* therapy. Further, the questions of how the working social order should be understood, and of what its key points are, are questions to which the answers may well differ from one country to another, especially as between countries at different stages of development. So that whatever program we adopt may well need for underdeveloped countries a different approach and a different set of assumptions, with a reconsideration of what are important questions in relation to stages of development.[73] Yet all this is merely the practical ground of what is also a cardinal principle, namely that the advance cataloguing of topics for legal research is not the whole of the problem. Much decisive knowledge is as likely to come from inquiry into areas chosen for no better reason than the interest of the inquirer.[74] Among the most crucial needs, on either level, are to recruit and secure the dedication of personnel of the necessary caliber, to make available the material means, and assure the conditions of free and continuing inquiry which will maintain that firm dedication.[75]

PROGRAM AND MOVEMENT
IN THE BORDERLANDS OF LAW AND
SOCIAL SCIENCE

I

AS LONG AGO as 1912 Roscoe Pound formulated in this mood a series of practical objectives for sociological jurisprudence in common-law countries.[1] This program in its time was a powerful prod of the attention of lawyers towards the relations of law and society, both on the side of methodology, and on that of *ad hoc* problems of adjustment and maladjustment of law. If we think of the assessment of such a program in terms of neat and complete performance, then even in 1943, when the present author was writing *The Province and Function of Law*, it seemed necessary to lament that the program remained both urgent and largely unexecuted. From the perspective of 1963, however, it has now become clear that this was unduly pessimistic.

For, first, the last two decades have shown a gathering of momentum and a widening range in this field of concern, even in the comparatively conservative British democracies, which put the methodological controversies and practical hesitations of earlier decades in a more favorable light. And second, it has also become clear that the directions of interest formerly thought of as especially associated with the sociological school have now become shared by all who are seriously concerned with understanding or amending the law. We need not make any final judgment as to how far this orientation is to be credited to the half-century-old sociological program itself, though clearly it is so in some substantial degree. It is certainly also due to the very pressures of social change, to the expansion of the range of legal intervention under the pressure of this and to electoral demands made more effective through party-political organization and competition. In any case (and this is the present point) I believe it now to be quite artificial to introduce the practical concerns of the study of law and society in terms of a *Programschrift*, as distinct from a sampling of lines of juristic activity already proceeding.

The need to readjust perspectives in this manner is increased by certain other considerations. One is that sociological jurisprudence, like any other outcropping of human thought, was itself a creature of a time and place, and its earlier scope and tenor were in part conditioned by this. Before World War I, when its work developed in the United States, the beginnings of social legislation and of a positive federal attitude towards economic institutions and their stability and progress were still struggling for legitimation in face of various social and economic ideologies, traditional common-law hostility to statutes, jealousy for states' rights, and the conceptualism and logicism shared with the followers of Austin in England and of the Pandectists on the European continent. The social evils to which statutes held unconstitutional were often a serious response, accelerated with accelerating industrial and economic change; so did the invocations of the federal commerce power against economic ills and abuses.

Stating the matter more generally, the maladjustment and inadequacies of the law for its contemporary tasks gave to early sociological jurisprudence an overwhelmingly activist drive which, even when it expressed itself in general terms, was in fact directed at *ad hoc* remedies for all the particular defaults of the legal order. A great deal of the work in this area even to the present day is still of this nature. And, of course, thus regarded such a program is inexhaustible, and its nonfulfillment even in a century of work is certain. In this sense the program was over-ambitious, and was thus still open to the charge of failure even after it had contributed to massive changes in the law and in attitudes towards it. As with engineers of other kinds, and especially the traffic engineer of a modern city, Pound's "social engineer" was certain to be a busy man, far behind in his work, however many and mighty the projects already completed.

Finally, it seems clearer now than it was in 1946 that movements of thought and action touching the relations of law and society, insofar as they move into more fruitful contact with other social sciences, must come to place more stress on the importance of cognition of the social and economic order in its complex unity. And this even when they are bent upon an approach to diagnosis and remedy of specific evils through legal action. Economic thought has come to approach the problems of human distress due to economic fluctuations through control of key points in an *understood* economic ordering, itself institutionally framed within the more comprehensive social order. Contemporary sociological thought, well illustrated as we shall shortly see in the aspirations of Parsons' later thought, seeks a framework of thought receptive of social data which will allow us to see "the social system" as an integrated equilibration of the multitude of operative systems of values and institutions embraced within it. Whatever the difficulties of the Parsonian efforts in this direction, we believe that some corresponding change of horizons is likely in sociological jurisprudence, as many of the more elementary and glaring legal maladjustments which provoked the activism of its initial program become corrected.

The change may indeed already have begun. We are, for example, no longer perplexed by the question of interfering with liberty of contract, when gross inequality of bargaining power makes abuse of liberty likely. It has been handled in an *ad hoc* way by legislating for specific relations like landlord and tenant or lender and borrower. We are, on the other hand, increasingly perplexed by such comparatively new and diffuse problems as that of the use of trade union pressure against non-members, pressure of capital concentrations against competitors and consumers, the steady growth of juvenile and urban delinquency, the creeping paralysis of traffic congestion in the spreading metropolis, chronic delays in the administration of justice, the adjustment of capital-labor relations and of habits of leisure and systems of education to the age of automation.

These are the more characteristic kinds of areas demanding legal action for the future of the Western democracies. No doubt some problems will continue to be thrown up for which the *ad hoc* approach of early sociological jurisprudence, making direct assault on the points where legal maladjustment is immediately manifest, is apt. But the sociological jurist of the future will also have to approach his characteristic problems through a vast effort at understanding the wider social context, seeking by the light of available social knowledge the key points of the systems of action from which adjustment can be effectively made. Nor indeed, is this likely development at too great odds with some aspects of the past aspirations of sociological jurisprudence. For a number of these, such as the demand that the necessary expertise for pre-legislative tasks be made available on a stable institutionalized base, are as relevant to the broad tasks of cognition as they are to the *ad hoc* tasks of legal activism.[2] So is the search, which has already produced crisis after crisis in the tasks of practitioners and courts, for more basic and meaningful categories of thought, for instance, in the law of damages for personal injuries, of liability for dangerous chattels and operations, of anti-trust law, of the law of economic association, and a score of others. And the impressive contemporary work of Willard Hurst in social and economic legal history [3] is in important part a search for categories of thought, drawn from empirical historical data, which will serve to put into the order of reason the interplay of legal and non-legal phenomena in the dimension of time.

IN AN IMPORTANT DEGREE, of course, all science including social science has as its central concern this search for more basic and meaningful categories. Certainly modern social science has moved away from any merely taxonomic view of its tasks. Its central problem has come to be that of seeing the social order as a functioning unity despite the multitude of its members, the apparent chaos of the constituent elements in their relations and the fact that birth and death and other biological events are constantly changing the membership. Most anthropologists and social scientists have come at present to accept the theory of the performance of social roles by members, after these have been somehow allocated among them, as central to whatever explanation as possible. Role theory is as important in Parsons' sociology as in the lamented S. F. Nadel's outstanding anthropological work; [4] and it remains so despite the need to guard against confusing its technical sense with the dramatic and literary associations of the word "role" in other contexts.[5]

The great value of the role notion, Nadel pointed out, lies in the fact that it provides a concept intermediary between "society" and "individual," facilitating our understanding of how individual behavior can become social conduct, and individual qualities and propensities can become social norms and values. The areas of such transition and translation are clearly of critical importance for all social science and for understanding law in relation to society. For it is obvious that society somehow rests on constancies of behavior of various kinds, including institutions or institutionalized modes of action, relationships, and groupings. The role notion allows us to analyze this complex situation into more refined terms of constituent tasks, goals, expectations, rights and duties, and the like, just as it allows us to see how social functions continue when the individuals in charge of them are always dying, and how the individual person may be a very plural unit in terms of roles in the social process.

The role notion is thus finally a way of thinking about those uniformities in society which are not *merely* uniformities in the sense of those studied by the physical sciences. But of course the characteristics of particular roles in a given society are to be found empirically and it is fairly common ground that the empirical evidence to be looked for is of three interconnected kinds. One is evidence of the frequency and regularity of the patterned concurrence of particular attributes of tasks and their performance, which gives a basis of statistical "normality" to the role series. The second consists of explicit converging statements of people (whose view is for some reasons thought reliable) as to the attributes appropriate to given roles. These, Nadel well observed, "are all value judgments, indicating the believed-in or desired 'normality,' and hence the normality codified." Third, evidence of the characteristics of concrete roles in a given society may be drawn from the way in which the various parts of the social order are geared to support the fulfillment of the roles and deter from deviance, in particular how and when its sanctioning machinery works. But of course concrete roles are also subject to change and therefore to confusion in the evidence. At some point deviants who still recognize the norm of their role may turn into non-conformists who are asserting *a changed norm*, and if they are persistent and numerous enough the normative attributes of the role may eventually have to be regarded as changed.[6]

In another aspect, the empirical evidence which gives precision to particular concrete roles also informs us concerning the tasks or functions which a particular society requires to be performed, and this is another way of saying that it tells us how the particular society chooses to commit its various resources. Insofar as the roles or complexes of roles which use these resources have to be filled by members of the society, the role-concept is also central for understanding the allocation of the members of the society to tasks and functions which are to be performed: this means in effect the allocation of members among the various roles. And insofar as some roles are more desired or desirable than others this also leads to inquiry and understanding as to the various criteria of eligibility for given roles which particular social systems recognize. It is further implicit in these allocations of human capacities and other social resources to the selected tasks and functions that the allocation of a person to a role is also an allocation of resources and other facilities *to him* for performance of the role. These facilities may be physical facilities. They also extend, however, to other facilities, designate in a broad sense as power. These include wealth, that is, economic resources which can be used to reward collaboration and are a means of acquiring further facilities; and power to activate or call on the collective support of the whole society in demanding that other persons collaborate either actively or by non-interference in the achievement of the purposes of the actor.[7]

III   One Role of Empirical investigation

TO OFFER a framework within which we can see the relations to each other of acts and ideas emergent from the structure and functioning of society is not of course to describe any particular society, much less to solve its problems. But it may be an important step towards both of these tasks. I shall make use of the framework offered by Parsons' *The Social System* in 1952, not because it can be regarded as in any way final, much less as beyond criticism, but rather as a sample of modern sociological theorizing focused on the social role notion. I shall make important criticisms of it from the jurisprudential standpoint. Yet it serves well enough as a sample of such theorizing not only because of its ambitious sweep, but because it seeks to accommodate the results of empirical research concerning facts of social life and the functions which emerge within it, as well as the results of non-empirical inquiries concerning the needs and values expressed in the social system. It has special interest for the theory of law, in its restatement (not always with awareness that it *is* a restatement) of important aspects of the existing sociological and jurisprudential standpoints, for instance, as to the meaning and import of *de facto* human claims, as to the meaning of group-will, of criminal behavior and retribution, not to speak of the tendencies of socio-ethical conviction and power to approach each other of which the legal order of a society may be a main manifestation.

I have already referred to the key concept at present favored for a systematic view of the structure and functions of a society, explaining the comparative orderliness amid the multifarious individual and group needs, demands, and attitudes as that of the social roles allocated, accepted, and performed by members of the society. The individual as a natural (psychological and physical) reality presents himself in the social order sometimes as a unity which may participate as such in decisions of the whole society, but more usually as a bundle of status-roles — of father, municipal voter, industrial worker, tenant, vendor, purchaser, and a hundred others.[8] Only some of these are in play in any particular social action; and one or more roles may be lost while the individual yet fully preserves his remaining roles, as well as his over-all personality as an individual.[9] And while in theory an individual's act may be built on his own personal need-dispositions, in the social process these need-dispositions become disciplined within a system of expected reactions from others. This system of expected reactions organizes itself around the tasks which emerge regularly to be done. The roles which a man plays arise from the recognition that the particular tasks are allocated to him. And each role carries with it facilities to the one who bears it, and likelihood of reactions from others to the exercise of these facilities. The likely reactions from the others in turn depend on the expectations which they attach to the role (the "role-expectations").

The cultural tradition of a society, in the broad anthropological sense, arises from two consequential processes. One is the tendency for choices of action in roles and role-expectations to come to mutual adaptation. The other is that this tendency carries with it the development of a prevailing language and symbolic system, in order to permit stability of the adaptations in time and as between different individuals.[10] The cultural tradition, in this sense, covering as it does men's expectations of each other in their several roles, means that a social system includes an order "imposed" on persons, and their acts and attitudes. That is to say: the mutuality of expectations, and the dependence of the role-bearer's gratifications on the others' reactions (and therefore the obligation to meet the role-expectations), are oriented towards the order embodied in the cultural tradition. This means that the three main foci of a social system, the individual actor, the interactive system, and a system of cultural patterning, as well as the normative orientation of action within it, are all comprehended together in the notion of social action. Further, the variability of each of these three foci is limited by its compatibility with the minimum conditions of functioning of each of the other two.[11] "The social system" is thus a kind of system of systems and sub-systems, systemic quality being manifest at each point in functional interdependence of parts and their tendency to equilibration and homeostasis in face of disturbance. In personality need-dispositions the balance wheel (as it were) is of gratification-deprivation: in society it is of reciprocal role-expectations; in culture it is of value patterns which provide the normative content of role-expectations in society, and of need-dispositions in personality. Each such major system has sub-systems for which it is the environment, and all these systems and sub-systems interpenetrate each other in the actual social process. For this to go on goals must be somehow approximated, adaptation made to changing environment, a degree of cohesion maintained, and the tensions incidental to all this kept to a tolerable level.[12]

This approach departs, obviously, from the view that cooperation and conformity within a social system are to be explained by "spontaneous" acts of members resulting from the independently determined characteristics of individuals. It rather sees the functioning of the social system, as Malinowski saw that of law in less developed societies, as resting on "relatively specific mechanisms, that is, modes of organisation of the motivational systems of personalities, which can be understood in direct relation to the socially structured level of role behaviour." Deviance from what is expected of *ego* sets up the reaction or probability of reaction of others to failure of the role-expectation, which may thus be regarded as a sanction of conformity built into the system. Role-expectations and sanctions in this sense are reciprocal to each other.[13] The existence of a social system means that this expectation-sanction interaction is not confined to any specific others or group of such, but that it arises with any other members of society *vis-à-vis* any role-bearer: in other words that role-expectations and the value standards they imply have become more or less institutionalized in the process of social interaction. Furthermore, the institutionalized expectations and values become, in their turn, internalized in the personality structure of members. In this manner "a genuine motivational integration of behaviour in the social structure takes place."[14] Personal motivation becomes harnessed in proportion as this proceeds, to the fulfillment of role-expectations and their ancillary value-standards.

This theorem of institutional and behavioral integration is reached deductively. It provides, however, a beginning point of reference from which it is then necessary (Parsons recognizes) to elaborate empirically detailed distinctions as to the modes (cognitive, cathectic, and evaluative) in which the individual's orientations are conditioned by internalization of culture patterns.[15] Or, putting the matter the other way, we need to see how the expectations institutionalized in the culture become internalized and patterned in the individual psychology of members. This elaboration Parsons attempts in some detail, and in particularly difficult terminology.[16] He is able, at any rate, to offer a schematic outline of how "Modes and Types of Action-Orientation" are interrelated with "Culture Patterns and Institutions." The three main modes of motivational orientation are reflected in three corresponding modes of value-orientation, and in three corresponding types of culture pattern, depending on which mode of orientation has primacy in the particular culture. By considering a motivational mode as combined with its corresponding type of culture pattern, we may discover the main types of "action interests," namely, in knowing, in adjustment to secure gratification, and in integration to resolve or minimize conflicts. On this basis Parsons then perceives a number of types of "evaluative action-orientation" directed either to the pursuit of goals ("instrumental") or to the expression by "acting out" of need-disposition; or to moral integration either of the actor or of the collectivity of which he is a member. Value-orientation patterns thus emerging may then become institutionalized in any of three main types. There are (1) *relational* institutions which define reciprocal role-expectations as such, independent of interest content; (2) *regulative* institutions (*including the legal and the moral*) which set limits as to goal and means for pursuit of "private" interest; and (3) *cultural* institutions, "defining obligations to acceptance of culture patterns" with the effect of converting private acceptance into institutionalized commitment.[17]

The long-term importance of such an attempt to provide an overall scientific frame of reference for the guidance of social research and the classification of its results is clear. For jurisprudence this is increased by Parsons' sensitive use of many ideas of writers like Durkheim, Freud, Pareto, and Weber which have already entered the stream of juristic thought. Despite their difficulties of formulation, even for specialists in social science, some of Parsons' basic notions cannot be neglected by jurisprudents. We must accordingly make certain observations on them from the juristic standpoint.

IV

THE COMPLEX SYSTEM of mutual adaptations of role-expectations and performances, of these to culture patterns (including *value* patterns), of cultural institutions to such patterns, and of the internal motivations of members of society to these institutions, and the refinements and combinations within these adaptations, constitute for Parsons the main dynamic within a social system. They are the source he thinks both of equilibrium and change within it; and he insists that for his theory social change is not a separate problem, but only a phase in the same dynamic of adaptation.[18]

He is concerned, however, not to assume that the content of a social system springs from some inherent quality in the particular society itself, giving premiums for favored types of adaptations and deterrents against those disfavored. What is important to him is, first, the mechanisms (which he conceives as including even a "belief-system") by which actors are under pressure to adapt their value- and action-orientations in an orderly or systematic fashion; and second, the propensity of individual actors to make these adaptations. This, it would seem, is the meaning of his rather inadequately explained notion of "need-dispositions" for what might otherwise be thought of as "basic needs." The use of the term seems to merge the idea of "need" with that of "propensity," suggesting that the individual's "needs" at any one time are not formed hard, but are constantly being molded in the dynamic network of social relations.[19]

Parsons has, however, been accused of begging the question whether a social system is by its nature capable of radical change.[20] It is certainly true that for him "the continuance of a stabilised motivational process in a stabilised relationship to the relevant objects is to be treated as not problematical." This is because (he thinks) the individual in each society learns his way gradually by way of equilibrating processes. For instance, he finds that performances have to be matched with expected gratifications, and adapted to the reactions of others. These processes (he admits) tend to "counteract tendencies to change the system." [21] Yet it is also an essential part of this same position that the real problems for sociology are the emergence, despite all this, of tendencies to change, alongside the counter-tendencies of the social system to keep pressure for change within limits. The central notion of "equilibrium" [22] implies that even such change as does occur occurs *within* the system, which (as it were) still maintains its boundaries. The equilibrium is a "moving equilibrium." Obviously limits on possible movement are here implied; and this is no doubt the reason for the charge that Parsons justifies the *status quo* by providing an elaborate rationalization of the impossibility of any *major* change in it.

For the analysis of demands and adaptations Parsons offers a series of contrasting characterizations to serve as "pattern variables." [23] The qualities referred to by the characterization represent choices which constantly present themselves to actors in the course of the social interaction process. Theoretically each member of each contrasting pair may be found in given situations in combination with any member of any of the other pairs. In fact certain combinations tend to be fairly constantly recurring, and others of the thirty-odd possible ones rarely or never occur. A question has also been raised of how far these "pattern variables" are overlapping.[24] However this be, it will be apparent as we proceed that the contrasts involved often have great potentialities for clarifying jurisprudential problems.

1. Affectivity / Affective Neutrality. Where an institution is based on affectivity, due performance of the resulting role requires the actor to adapt himself (in his temperament and emotions) to persons or situations, in the way, for example, in which as all of us will readily understand that law and morals demand adaptation by a parent or a spouse. Where it is based on "affective neutrality," as with lawyer and client, or bookseller and customer, or judge and litigant or juryman, or policeman and citizen, the commitment of attention and emotion is more limited and disciplined. An emotive adaptation in such latter roles may even be improper or obstructive to adequate role performance.

2. Diffuseness / Specificity. The affectivity / affective neutrality dichotomy is often closely related in the actor's choice with that of "diffuseness-specificity." This latter distinction, which will remind the lawyer of his own hoary *in rem–in personam* distinction, turns on whether (as in diffuseness) the whole personality of the actor is more or less indefinitely committed, or (as with specificity) only part of his personality and that only for a limited time is involved in a role-relationship. At the latter extreme would be the role of salesgirl *vis-à-vis* a casual customer, at the former the reciprocal roles of parent and child, and lifelong friends to each other. While affectivity and diffuseness more usually go together to reinforce each other, the alternate combination may occur with correspondingly modified results.[25]

3. *Universalism / Particularism.*[26] While the preceding dichotomies may be present even in interpersonal relations short of the wider society which is their locus, that between universalism and particularism turns specifically on demands pressed for the whole society. A man's relation is particular as with a friend, or kinsman, or member of his family, as to whom in varying degrees it may be expected or even demanded of him that he shall prefer them to all others, regardless of merit. The relation is universalist when the role from which it arises forbids such preferences and requires that precedence be given to capacity, honesty, usefulness, beauty, or whatever else be the qualification which is relevant to the action. It would be dysfunctional for the judge of a beauty competition to prefer his wife because she is his wife. But after the show is over it is his wife whom he should take home.[27]

4. *Quality / Performance.*[28] Choice according to performance means according to *expectation* of performance, though this may be based on past performance. The contrast is with quality in the sense rather of status or ascribed quality, of which birth status is the best known but not the only possible type. The distinction between more static societies (based on status or ascribed quality) and mobile societies (based on performance) is, of course, a main interest of sociology. It is well recognized that social systems commonly make use of both bases for allocation of roles, though there is a tendency in highly industrialized society for the performance basis to press back the status basis.[29]

5. *Collectivity-Orientation / Self-Orientation.* Only superficially similar to the universalist-particularist distinction is that between roles like those of physician or legal adviser, public servant or political leader where the interests of some more or less wide collectivity demand to be regarded;[30] and "self-oriented" roles (such as those of the parties to a contract negotiation) where the bearer is expected to look after his own interest.

Such pairs of contrasts can serve as "pattern variables" by reference to which we can more precisely characterize relations arising from cultural, including legal, institutions. They do not fully reveal "natural laws" which determine processes within the social system, but rather help to bridge gaps in knowledge by a kind of checklist function. If borne in mind as we recanvass many branches of the law, for instance of trustees, family relations, agency, of duty in the law of torts, privilege in defamation, they may also help to improve our formulations of legal principles. In the legal as in the wider social order, the fixing of the variables apposite to particular institutions or relations comes to be empirically determined. As this occurs other characteristics are indicated which are entailed in such variables.[31] If a certain kinship structure dominates in a particular society, so that it is organized predominantly on "quality" or "status" rather than "performance," the range of variations in the system pattern as to many other matters may become much less at random. For instance a jurist confronted with such a society will expect to find the range of specific–particularist–self-oriented relations (e.g., the right and practice of liberty of contract) comparatively limited; and he will also expect commerce not to be at a high level of activity. By fixing certain of these variables in the society the existence of other particular features of a legal order may thus be rendered more probable. The whole apparatus is in Parsons' own view not strictly a theory, but rather a "paradigm" or model, which suggests what else we should look for. It thus relieves us of the hazards of looking for the significant completely *at random*, as was too often done in the search for the "laws of natural selection" by many exponents of Social Darwinism.[32] In short when we have fixed empirically *some* of these variables at a given time and place, we have also often determined other features of the society which are known usually to accompany or depend on them.

V

THE LACONICALLY INVOLUTED and esoteric language of Parsons' theorizing [33] should not conceal that much of it is resolvable into half a dozen or so fundamentally simple notions. Thus, first (it may be said) a large amount of social action of humans is *goal-directed*. Second, social action is sufficiently patterned to allow for analysis in terms of *systems*. Third, man's command of symbolization enables him to generalize from experience and to stabilize patterns of behavior through time, this being the essence of what is meant by institutionalization of the patterns. It is implied in this third point that simple stimulus-response interpretations, in which meaning is contingent on the particular situation, are inadequate to account for highly elaborate action systems. Correspondingly, symbolization is no mere adornment or idiosyncrasy of social life, but is a means of achieving a degree of abstraction and of escaping from the particularities in social action and its interpretation. Fourth, human action is, in part, directed by orientation to value-standards. Fifth, action-systems represent "compromises" rather than "perfect integration" among organismic, cultural, personality, and social systems, as motivated actors contend with the exigencies of survival in an environment.[34] On an even more common-sense level it can be added that when we deal with others we must and usually do take account of what they expect of us, and that there are lasting patterns in the way people behave.

In adding these last and some other simple paraphrases [35] Professor Black has wondered "whether it is plausible for fundamental social theory to be so close to commonsense." But the question is obviously rhetorical. For there is no reason why the precepts of common sense, empirically learned, should not by statement in appropriately meticulous terms, after further testing and refinement, supply some of the framework for accumulating and systematizing further empirical knowledge. And this is true in the general social as in the jurisprudential field.[36]

From this latter standpoint we find it regrettable that this notable theorizing about the nature and structure of a social system should have been so neglectful of the jurisprudential (and even sometimes of the common) knowledge of lawyers. Neither in his own main works, nor in notable recent scholarly discussions concerning these, do contributions from the juristic side, even in its modern sociological emphasis, appear to have played any part. Yet in few areas of social study have the mechanisms of social control and gradual social change or (for that matter) the notions of a system of institutionalized expectations and value-orientations and processes of compromise, and the very notions of system and equilibrium themselves, been longer under discussion.

Parsons, for example, observes of a social system that since it is "a system of processes of interaction between actors, it is the structure of the *relations* between the actors as involved in the interactive process which is essentially the structure of the social system." [37] If we substituted the words "legal order" for "social system," we would have a parallel basic statement which all jurists and even most lawyers would immediately recognize not only as true but even as commonplace. In no other body of thought, too, is the notion of sanctions (including social-psychological sanctions) more central. A similar point must be made as to the role-performance notion. Parsons attempts to base his relational analysis of institutions and role-expectation on what he regards as the "key concept" of the "division of labor" as developed by Adam Smith and his successors in utilitarian, and especially economic, theory. In fact, of course, the concept is an elementary legal concept. The whole notion of the legitimacy of demands as dependent on such particular role-relations as feudal lord and liege, landlord and tenant, vendor and purchaser, mortgagor and mortgagee, master and apprentice, trustee and *cestui que trust*, life tenant and reversioner, husband and wife, is central to the classical centuries of the common law and has now had a notable revival and metamorphosis to meet the problems of modern complex economically organized democratic polities.[38]

A most striking example of the sacrifice of mutual benefit by such lack of communication between social scientists and jurists and jurisprudents is to be found in some aspects of Parsons' treatment of the family, and in particular of the parent-child relations.[39] Parsons naturally finds in the family splendid illustrations for characterizing relations (here in terms of affectivity, diffuseness, and particularism) between roles and stable expectations, and between value-orientations and motivations anchored in them. And of course it provides examples par excellence of the ascription of roles (of father or mother) without any criterion based on prospective performance. It is also an illuminatingly obvious example of a sub-system which may change even within a relatively stable larger social system. Changes in it are indeed compelled not only by adaptation of the action of the role-performers — husband, wife, parent, child — but also by what are termed "non-action variables," namely, the physical life cycles of all the role-performers. The family, indeed, is a changing system one function of which is precisely to prepare the child to *leave* it; and as he moves towards this the role of both parent and child change. Its equilibration is thus supremely a moving dynamic equilibration.

All this in its turn is affected by interactive processes between the family sub-system and other sub-systems as well as by changes in the social system as a whole, such as those brought about by modern industry, science, and technology. For example, in the former cottage industry, of which an analogue is still found in Japan, the family unit of production was ancillary to the affectivity-diffuseness relations of the family. Modern factory industry has cut away this production aspect from the family: and in agricultural production, where the family is still important, less and less of the work force is engaged. People "go out to work" and work is done in patterns rather of the universalism-specificity-achievement type. This greater family isolation has different and sometimes conflicting effects on the role of the wife. Partly it accentuates her sex role, expressed in the glamor pattern; partly, in beckoning careers or other outside activities, it spells a break-out from the exclusive affectivity-diffuseness of her family role into roles of a universal-specific nature. Sometimes underlining, sometimes hindering these adjustments is the fading of the human variety and the rise of the mechanical variety of domestic help.

In this context Parsons has made a capital point concerning adequacy in the parental role. On the one hand, the ascriptive nature of the role and its affectivity and diffuseness demand that the *love* extended to the child shall be *unconditional*. On the other hand, the fact that this role arises in a system in which the growing child must be trained for independent social living requires that the *approval* by the parent of the child's specific performances shall be *conditional*; there can otherwise be no effective reward mechanism. Unless, therefore, the parent is able, in his relations with the child, to keep clear that the withholding of approval because of the child's failure to meet parental expectations of performance leaves the parental love still unconditional, disturbance and other pathogenic consequences in the child may have to be expected.[40]

At no point in his study does Parsons refer to the fact that at the law school of his own university, Sheldon and Eleanor Glueck had published two years before (in 1950), empirically based conclusions which confirmed his own rather deductively based hypothesis. This was that non-delinquent children were much more afflicted than delinquent children by fears and anxieties of loss of parental love. This was found to be so even with such non-delinquent children who had no reason either objectively speaking or in their own conscious understanding, to think that they had given ground for this loss.[41] A far better explanation of this fact than any offered by the Gluecks themselves is one which could well have emerged from Parsons' closely related thought, confirming both his and the Gluecks' positions. This is that the continuance of parental love is essential to keep viable such ascriptive, affectively diffuse roles as those of parent and child. Children who have this love will fear to lose it; *those who do not have it* (and this is the key point) *will not fear to lose it*.[42] And when the Gluecks' empirical evidence is added showing that parental love is an important crime-preventing factor, the fact that non-delinquent fear of the loss of it seems greater than that of delinquents is quite consistent. The empirical material when interpreted in the light of the elaboration of Parsons' role-expectation and role-fulfillment notions, thus yields important guidance both for parents and those concerned with social problems of delinquency.[43] It is obvious that defaults in making such fruitful cross-reference are wasteful and regrettable.[44]

This example also affords another warning for all workers in the social sciences. Compared to the Parsonian system-building, work on delinquent children designed to contribute to the practical tasks of courts and other social agencies may be regarded as empirical in method and *ad hoc* in motivation. I believe it to be of capital importance that the social sciences, and above all those bearing on problems of legal ordering, should not commit themselves *wholly and exclusively* to building over-all systems of thought, leaving it more or less to chance whether in the testing and elucidation of the theoretical principles involved the practical and sometimes gravely urgent problems of contemporary society are ever reached. We have already made clear that the drive to over-all cognition and theory-building represents a salutary trend in the social sciences, and promises in the long run great improvements in man's self-control and social control. There are, however, at least two compelling reasons why we dare not commit *all* our best expertise to the building and testing of over-all theories; and why indeed, those who guide research activity should take steps to avoid this excessive commitment.

One reason is that the advancement of cognition itself requires a continual checking of over-all theory by reliable empirical data collected and verified out of the matrix and even unconsciously of that theory. This is even more so in the social sciences where for a variety of reasons the exact empirical testing of hypotheses by experimentation tailored to the hypotheses is possible only to a much lesser extent than in natural sciences. The flow of data and hypotheses from particular problem areas still at a distance from the reach of theory is a correspondingly precious source of confirmation, correction, and supplementation which should not be allowed to dry up.

The other reason, no less compelling, proceeds from the view which I take (but which not all my colleagues may share) concern-

ing the responsibility of the social scientist (including the juris-
prudent) towards the tasks of legal ordering. And it would be
compelling even if in terms of the first reason the extension of
knowledge were not involved. I have already briefly mentioned this
second reason in my first essay. It is that in relation to legal ordering we are entitled to expect the assistance of social scientists in the
alleviation of practical evils and the handling of practical problems. And we are entitled to this, not only in the long run but (so
far as it *can* be made available) here and now. For generally some
action-response must be made by citizens, lawyers, judges, and ad-
ministrations in the here and now to these evils and these problems;
and the response ought to be as adequate as our generation's state
of knowledge can make it. We have already noted and welcomed
the tendency for sociological jurisprudence to take a wider and
more theoretical view of its subject-matter than it did in its pioneering decades from the turn of the century. We wish also now to
insist, however, that sociological jurisprudence (under whatever
name) should also strive to maintain its earlier courage and vigor
in tackling the numerous situations of obvious conflict, distress,
confusion and injustice which are thrown up constantly and ur-
gently for practical handling. We must enable and even encourage
scholars to address themselves to these without making them feel
that they have wandered from the main roads of scholarship, or
that their activity is any less respectable or important than the
building or criticism or testing of over-all theoretical systems.

Returning now to the more general level of a contribution to the
fundamental theory of society, perhaps the deepest difficulty with
Parsons' positions lies in the fact (already adverted to) that it depends so much at critical points on the central notion of "equilibrium." R. M. Williams has observed [45] that not only is this notion
insufficiently explained, but that even so far as explained it is not
present as a constant force. Insofar as this is so there may have been
a strong temptation even for so sophisticated a mind as Parsons' to
give it the functions of a *deus ex machina*, especially for the problems of social change. Yet it must also be said in fairness that the

problem Parsons set himself was not to provide a framework which would receive *everything that might happen* to a given society, *including traumatic change and breakdown.* His frame was rather to accommodate (and admirably so) what went on in society *as long as it was a stable, going society,* that is, as long as it was not subjected to such blows. Yet even as we make this defense of Parsons we have to add that students of law as a social phenomenon, especially in an age of dynamic change like the present, must also try to understand the processes involved in traumatic change and breakdown in the legal and social orders. And it is to be hoped that as this kind of concern comes to engage general social theory the accumulated data and ideas from the juristic side will receive due attention from sociologists.

Linked with this criticism of the "equilibrium" notion is the view that the general trend of Parsons' theories is to soften the actualities of coercion and conflict with the balm-like qualities of the notions of "adaptation" and "integration." Yet here again on both points the jurists' dissatisfactions may be rather less.[46] For, however it be with social systems as a whole, Parsons would be entitled to say that the legal system is an "integrative sub-system" of society, and that the integrative function at least assumes that some minimal harmony of role-expectations, such as Parsons has taken for granted, survives whatever disintegrative forces are at work.[47]

VI

IN VENTURING THUS, from the jurisprudential standpoint, on certain criticisms of this notable sample of contemporary social theory and science I do not intend to stake or restake any claim for the establishment of a "social science of law" or "sociology of law" as an autonomous branch of social science parallel to economics, anthropology, social psychology, and the rest. My own position has been and remains that in terms of knowledge (as distinct from the practical convenience of marshaling it for legal purposes) the principles known or to be discovered concerning the role of law in society ought already to be within the proper scope of concern of other social sciences.[48] For such principles only describe, in the final analysis, the adjustments and interactions between physical, social economic, cultural, and spiritual environments, and the psychological processes which lie behind the origins, institutionalizations, and manipulations of power and submission to it, order, ethical and other values accepted, and the like. As such their discovery and elaboration is the concern of the various existing social sciences which should (as we have said) try to make more adequate use of legal data, so that their conclusions may be of maximum value both to knowledge generally, and to jurisprudence in particular.

The different view has been nevertheless pressed that a distinct social science might concern itself with the nature and operation of those special combinations and interactions of social, economic, and political institutions and processes generally associated with the law.[49] Thus, on Parsons' stimulating classification,[50] the "analytical sciences of social action" would be mainly three: economics (dealing with "economic rationality"), politics (dealing with "coercive rationality"), and sociology (dealing with social action systems so far as understandable in terms of "common-value integration"). But in addition there would be a number of technologies dealing with the "concrete content of immediate ends, norms and knowledge," of which that touching the "legal" might well be one.

Whether or not a distinct "social science" of law is philosophically defensible in these or any other terms, I do wish to insist in closing that it is at least necessary to maintain the study of law and society as an identifiable field of study under the aegis of jurisprudence, if only for practical purposes deriving from the technical nature of legal materials and the needs of legal education. First, the esoteric nature of the law means that the social scientist not trained as a lawyer is likely to encounter formidable obstacles in handling legal materials as part of the subject-matter of his own branch of knowledge. Recognition of the separate jurisprudential field draws attention to the special difficulty of handling the materials. Second, the law by its nature cuts across almost all the conceivable subjects of social science. The "legal" fairly infests the culture.[51] Even more perhaps than with other social sciences the study of law as a part of the social process involves, above all, integration — a sort of specialization in non-specialization. Third, the need in legal education for an orderly view of the law's "external relations" is particularly pressing so far as its social relations are concerned.[52] From the pedagogical viewpoint, if the study of the operation of law in society as an identifiable (though not autonomous) subject did not exist, it might be necessary to invent it.[53]

What is here asserted is the *practical* need, in view of these considerations, to recognize a branch of study in which lawyer expertise and social science expertise may exchange data and hypotheses, and become aware of the main movements in their related areas. From the present juristic standpoint what is important is to maintain channels whereby the study of law in society may be steadily informed by learning derived from the social sciences. And this is to be stressed even though, after decades of more ambitious manifestoes, it still seems safer to reserve our position as to integration and unification of the social sciences *inter se*, and as to proposals for integration of the study of law into the social sciences, and sometimes even for "law" itself to become a "social science." There is no harm, however, in referring to this liaison of juristic and social science concerns as "interdisciplinary" provided we do not thereby stir illusions of jurisprudential grandeur. As with other branches of jurisprudence, the sociological is concerned to study law in its relation with other disciplines — here the social sciences. In particular it seeks to illuminate the empirical data of law by concepts and ideas drawn from the social sciences, and to give reciprocal aid to the social sciences. This exchange may even extend to some of the concepts and hypotheses developed respectively in jurisprudential and social science work. Here too the study of law is more likely to be the gainer, though we may recall that the phenomena of imitation and diffusion of institutions became subjects of jurisprudential concern at least as early as any social science addressed itself to them. The limits of prudence are probably reached, however, before we begin speculating whether we can hope that jurisprudence and the social sciences may be able to unify their respective theoretical frameworks, and bring this unified framework to bear on the investigation of the same empirical problems.[54]

+

MAN AND MACHINE
IN THE SEARCH FOR JUSTICE
OR WHY APPELLATE JUDGES
SHOULD STAY HUMAN

IN MY CONCLUDING ESSAY I must try to reward the reader's patience with earlier generalities by speaking of some more concrete concerns in the contemporary administration of justice. From the multitude available I have selected one group; in doing so I have had regard to four criteria. The first is the degree of importance for the whole legal order of the institution whose problematics are involved. The second is the degree of urgency of better understanding and handling of these problematics. The third is the degree to which these are likely to baffle us, unless we have adequate understanding and support from other branches of knowledge including the social sciences. The fourth is the extent to which the field of legal activity concerned, that of legal advising and adjudication, is already feeling pressures from technological developments and from work in the social and political sciences. I have in mind the bearings of computer technology on legal tasks, on the one hand, and, on the other, the bearings on legal tasks of political scientists' ventures into the quantitative analysis of judicial behavior. And the lines of my concern are hinted at in both of my titles: "Man and Machine in the Search for Justice," or "Why Appellate Judges Should Stay Human."

I

THE CONFRONTATION of human perplexities with machine potentialities has now moved on to a broad front, even if we think only of lawyers' concerns.[1] We can already list many of the issues around which battle is to rage. Do the activities of computers especially in alliance with the assumptions of behavioral science express a philosophy (and also express it in a language) irreconcilably alien to the great traditions of law? Is the fear justified that technology demands for its efficient use closed logical systems which would hamstring the growth of a legal order which had to be contained within them? Would lawyers' acceptance of the great services which these new techniques may offer spell abdication of professional legal skills? Would the desiderata of precision of concepts and language often thought to be required for the machines tend to make lawyers despise and reject the semantic fertility of legal language? Would the very technological ability of machines to handle complex and massive data, if we indulged it, tend to produce over-refinement and over-complexity of legal prescriptions? Would it become a means, when harnessed to expanding governmental powers, of accelerating the already rapidly growing subjection of citizens to centralized bureaucratic and technocratic power?

Such questions can be extended and multiplied and given ever more dramatic forms.[2] An undercurrent of hostility to traditional lawyerdom as a self-centered and defensive craft and an enemy of the extension of knowledge may be felt even in those protagonists of behavioralism and machine techniques who do not aspire to enthrone multivariate calculations in the very seat of justice. Even among those who try to see both sides, conclusions sometimes outrun prudence to allege that suggested limitations on machine potentialities for the tasks of law and justice may rest merely on the accidents of legal history and on the practical limitations of legal craftsmanship hitherto.[3] The blockages to communication which result from such overstatements are not removed by subsequent assertions of confidence that machines "will remain our servants and not become our soulless masters."

It is no less unhelpful when such overstatements attack rather than defend the newer approaches. It may be interesting to speculate with T. L. Becker [4] whether intemperance in curiosity spurred by new investigative techniques and instruments may result in indiscriminate studies in areas where only harm to social institutions may ensue, and whether there should not be some organs to determine the strategy and priorities among researches which raise such dangers. So Carl F. Stover [5] has warned equally broadly that the new methods, far from freeing the lawyer's (including presumably the judge's) time for "higher questions" may enslave it to "routinized" formulas. So that ideas like that of justice, whose richness and ambiguities are somehow essential for dealing with the human situation, may (if we are not rather deliberate about it) receive even less attention than in the past. And W. Berns has generalized the charge that behavioralist work, denying as it does any concern with the value-elements in judicial decision, must involve dangers of excessive weighting of purportedly value-free "scientific" data.[6]

From the standpoint of an economist J. J. Spengler has sustained a thesis that a result of reducing problems of law and justice to forms permitting machines to handle them would be to increase the range of constraint on individuals above the necessary minimum, and that the expansive role of the modern state would tend rapidly to aggravate this tendency.[7] He is concerned, too, to stress the uniqueness of each legal and judicial problem and the inaptness of machines for handling problems involving unique elements. All this would represent the new developments in terms of a rather oversimple struggle between standardizing techniques and the legal needs of individualization. The effect of taking such wide canvases must, we believe, be to present as unnecessarily broad such conflicts as there may be between electronic techniques and traditional legal methods. And this is no more adequate as a basis of dialogue than sweeping contrary theses that there is no "funda-mental irreconcilable hostility between law and technology." [8]

These wide questionings are from within the ranks of political and social scientists themselves, reflecting their own domestic po-lemics between traditionalism and behavioralism. We are naturally not surprised to find numerous cries of alarm from the ranks of law-yers, no less general and unhelpful by their generality, and we have referred to many of these in the opening paragraph.[9] We believe that the better paths for future debate must be such as will allow us fully to acknowledge the wide range of potential services to the law of electronic devices and behavioralist methods. And this con-versely also requires us to delimit precisely if we can areas of legal tasks for which these are inapt, especially where inadvertence to the limits may inflict serious harm on legal ordering. Accordingly, against certain background problems of semantic change in lan-guage and of the judicial institution, and of the notable recent work on judicial behavior, this essay concerns itself to identify one such area. This is the area of appellate decision-making of a law-creative kind; we intend to ask for recognition of its special nature as well from those engaged in quantitative analysis of judicial behavior as from those who oppose this kind of work.

This area, though we shall show it to be critical for the function-ing of a legal order, does not embrace all appellate decision-mak-ing, much less decision-making at all levels. It embraces that part in which decisions have to be made as to whether law shall be modified by the judicial act, and if so, how much and in what direction. This area which I may here designate as the area of "the judgment of justice," lies at first sight rather near the central preoccupation of the pioneering work of Glendon Schubert and others in prediction of judicial behavior on the basis of quantitative analysis of past performance. It may even be that a great deal of controversy surrounding this work arises from lawyers' too easy as-sumptions that prediction of appellate decisions purporting to proceed on factorization independently of notions of "justice" is a threat to whatever that notion may stand for. This certainly is the mood of T. A. Cowan's observation with reference to such work on Supreme Court decisions, that lawyers "are hardly prepared to turn that august body into a group of experimental subjects to test the results of factor analysis." [10] It will be a main task here to articulate what reality may lie behind this feeling of "threat," sufficiently to allow clarifying discussion between opposing standpoints.

Despite the appearance of proximity between the prediction of decisions and the making of them, and despite juristic critics of the behavioralist search for reliable quantitative bases of prediction, the behavioralists may have no conscious designs whatsoever on the integrity of the decisional process. It may be that from their standpoint what we have called the judgment of justice, as a decision now about to be made by this judge, is of no concern at all. In his pioneer work of 1959, indeed, Glendon Schubert expressly states this self-limitation.[11] Certainly we ourselves tend thus to read the pioneers of this kind of scientific method as applied to the judicial process. Even when they are at their most sanguine about the effective use of multivariate analysis of objective factors, they are (as it seems to me) disposed to say that the question how the judge, the man in the judgment seat, *ought* to decide a given case (where this "ought" refers to the general norms of justice) is not susceptible to their methods.[12] Or perhaps they would say that they are simply not interested in this question. What concerns them is rather to discover how and why it is that judges of particular backgrounds have tended to decide particular kinds of past cases in the way they have, and with the question how far hypotheses can be framed which can serve as a basis for predicting future decisions — that is, predicting what these decisions *will be*, not what they *ought to be*.

Glendon Schubert, for instance, devotes a section of a recent exposé [13] to the very question: "Why is prediction important?" The answer he gives appears to have no bearing at all on the doing of justice in future judgments nor to the effects, good or bad, of accurate prediction of past judicial behavior on future acts of judgment. His focal concern is to show that behavioralists' prediction is better in various ways, above all by its reproducibility and the communicability of its methods, than prediction by even the most experienced and perceptive lawyer. And no doubt he would be inclined to elaborate that his concern is with the search for scientific "laws" governing judicial decision-making, so that neither the direct search for justice itself, nor the effects of the discovery of such "laws" by behavioralists on the judgment of justice or on the judicial institution, was the behavioralists' responsibility, any more than the incidence of a nuclear war would be a nuclear scientist's responsibility.[14] The scientific indifference here asserted is twofold. One is as to the question how the judge *should* proceed in making his judgment of justice now or in the future. The other is as to the "feedback" or "Heisenberg effect" of scientific prediction on future decisions as to justice as they will be made at the judgment seat, even when the judge is quite inadvertent to these.

We believe it important to observe that scientific indifference should not be stigmatized as necessarily irresponsible towards these aspects. We stress this not only because such terms rapidly lead to polemics, but even more because the correctness of such attitudes of indifference is more easily the subject of fruitful examination if we do not beg the question. Indifference rather than irresponsibility to the judgment of justice also appears to be the correct characterization of S. S. Ulmer's approach. He is content to conclude his latest article with the claim, not that scientific methods of the computer-behavioralist kind can provide answers to legal questions, but only that they "can improve significantly the analytical powers of those who use them." [15] And other recent writers,[16] after describing the esoterics of "modern logical skills" necessary for clarifying even the merely syntactic aspects of decisions, are content to declare (and in one breath) that they cannot hope to get many lawyers to acquire these particular skills, and that the problems on which these particular skills are focused are not even "the most important lawyer use of logical skills."

This preliminary caveat being laid against juristic misunderstanding of the intellectual drive of those devoting themselves to quantitative behavioral study of the judicial process, we must (to equalize our own peril) also address certain preliminaries to the victims of this misunderstanding. We venture to endorse, in particular, certain monitions recently addressed by a leading sociologist [17] to his colleagues, and to think that these may also have some application in the present field as well. The first is that a valid generalization in the social field requires more than *hic et nunc* postures, and it should take into account also the historical and comparative dimensions of the phenomena. Second, it is essential for us to be aware of the work of those who have addressed themselves to similar problems, and to existing theory which affects these problems even when these have arisen in a different field of social science than that which engages us. "Rediscovering America" or "reinventing the wheel" is not a fruitful activity even if we do it with new language and techniques. Third, methodology and new technical devices should not be allowed to dictate direction of interest without due regard to the importance or novelty of problems addressed. And this is applicable to mathematicization, as to other methods. "Measure by all means, measure, and count by all means, count. But let us count and measure the things that count." [18]

II

IN ORDER TO approach our core problems, surrounding the role of appellate judge in law-creation and development, we must first reconnoiter and traverse two regions. One is the terrain of language and its nature, central in which is its liability to semantic plurisignation and change, with all the implications that these have for operations with the authoritative materials of the law. The second is the terrain of judicial discretion and judicial choice-making wherein the legal order must be kept stable and moving, and the nature and limits of the judge's responsibility for the choices he makes must be confronted. Recognition of this latter terrain led some American realists three or four decades ago to challenge the decisiveness or even relevance of judicial reasoning and of supposed legal propositions for judicial decision-making; and led others, like the late Jerome Frank, to campaign for re-education of judges to fit them, by psychoanalytical and other methods, for intense self-awareness in the exercise of these choices.[19] These latter problems of judicial choice-making and responsibility are sufficiently familiar to most of us. But I must pause to speak of the semantic frame of legal prescription and discourse which here concerns us.

Overlaying and interweaving with a multiplicity of elements are two dimensions of a legal order, the linguistic and the argumentational. We confront these whenever we try to operate within it. On the one hand, language is the ubiquitous clothing of legal phenomena; on the other hand, logic and other forms of reasoning affect the way in which language is worked with and worked on to keep a legal system somehow viable and adaptable in face of constant change in its application to the social phenomena it seeks to regulate.

We are here concerned with the role of language. Obviously, better understanding of the operation of language is essential for clarifying all legal problems. For these are almost always concerned in some degree with a subject-matter (statements of or about law) encased or packaged for easy conveyance in linguistic communications, and to be unwrapped (as it were) by resort to still further linguistic communications. What is implied in this is the need to attend to (1) the relations between words as linguistic signs [20] and what they refer to ("semantics" in the narrow sense); (2) the formal relations of words to other words ("syntactics"); and (3) the relation of words with those who utter or receive or understand them ("pragmatics").[21] And while the word, as the minimum expression of meaningful content,[22] is the basic unit of communication by linguistic signs (or "discourse"), discourse generally requires a sentence, in which the syntactic relation of words to each other permits us to select among the multiplicity of meanings of each word so as to delimit somewhat what is communicated.

The word itself, as the basic unit of meaning, is semantically of triple function. First, the collocation of sounds or marks serves as a *symbol*. Second, the *symbol* signifies a certain thought or idea in the user's mind, the *reference* or *significatum*.[23] Third, the symbol itself and the thought or idea which is its *reference* or *significatum* must (or may) [24] refer to some other entity, the *referent* or *designatum*.[25] The word "cat" made up of certain sounds or marks is a symbol having as a *reference* the idea which this word expresses, and as a *referent* [26] the animal which corresponds to that idea. This is the simplest case. But it is also probably the general (though by no means unanimous) view that words can be meaningful even though not referring to "things" in this ordinary sense. Words are deemed meaningful for example when they refer to the speaker's own sensations, as his toothache or drowsiness. Words of disjunction and conjunction (such as "or" or "and"), which seem quite to lack a referent,[27] are seen as receiving their meaning directly from usage.[28] They are "logical" words, which tell us, for example, whether the rules of disjunction or conjunction apply to the words which they combine.[29] Some words, like "justice," are not even syntactic in function, nor do they stand for any entity apprehensible through the senses. The word or symbol here represents an abstraction, and if it is to have a referent, this must be found in traditional usage which designates the "thing meant," in what the medievals called *intentio intenta*, or the *pensée pensée*.[30]

The semantic teaching that words have many meanings, so that meaning can only be delimited contextually and syntactically, goes far beyond the commonplace that some words are ambiguous. For it means that no single meaning that is both determinate and stable can usually be fixed on any word; plurisignation [31] (or polysemy) is a pervading quality of words. No doubt there can be an ordinary meaning in a given context as A. H. Gardiner argues,[32] but the context changes with time, and with all that time changes.[33]

This bears upon the value of the still widely accepted principle of interpretation of legislation, including codes, which would make the legislator's will or intention the exclusive source of law; with the rider that "if the text of the code was clear in its ordinary meaning, that will was found in literal interpretation of the words." [34] I am not here concerned with the factual difficulties in this notion of "will" of the legislator — for instance with the truth of the assumptions that the many legislators have a collective will with common content, or that even those who vote for a code do will the contents as distinct from merely giving blanket approval to what others have drafted,[35] or that they could, however hard they tried, lay out precisely what is the law on all matters at a given time. We leave aside also the puzzle whether, if the principle were taken seriously, the court should seek the legislative will as it is found through the ordinary meaning of the words as they are understood when the statute is passed, or at the later time (possibly centuries later) when the question of interpretation arises. We are concerned here solely with the semantic aspects.

First, then, whatever a legislator may do, semantic considerations indicate that he cannot fix the "ordinary" meaning to be found by literal interpretation for all future interpreters.[36] The words of his code which are in common usage are subject to the principle of plurisignation when first used, and to semantic change with the flux of time in which language as a social phenomenon par excellence moves. No doubt some limits can be set to the plurality of meanings by careful use of words, and particularly of technical legal terms with less changeable traditional areas of meaning. Even in lawyers' discourse, however, a word is rarely unisignative and wholly unchangeable. Moreover, no statute could consist entirely of technical legal terms, and the canon prescribing the literal interpretation according to the ordinary meaning is in any case not applicable to such technical terms.

The deeper point here is that the precept as to the "will" or "intention" of the legislator, and the rider as to the "ordinary" meaning, can rarely be applied together as one directive. In cases of doubt, one or the other will usually fall by the way; this semantic truth reinforces what we shall later have to say concerning the frequently fictitious nature of judicial invocation of the legislative "will" or "intention." [37] We shall, indeed, have occasion to point this out in logical terms as to the British practice of excluding reference to the legislative proceedings which led up to the statute. This exclusion makes quite patent that the frequent judicial reference to the "intention" of the legislator will, at a pinch, be held to amount to no more than some kind of "objective" meaning *which can be given* to the words which the legislator used.[38]

It is now, indeed, widely accepted that it is a fallacy ("the intentionalist fallacy") to seek the meaning of written discourse in the will or intention of the author.[39] The British rule excluding *travaux préparatoires* makes more sense in terms of this semantic doctrine, than of the courts' own lip-service to the intention of the legislator.[40] Clearly, study of such *travaux* would be essential for seeking his "will" or "intention." Historians or sociologists, for example, must thus seek the motives of enactment; but lawyer and judge are concerned (so the British rule assumes) not with these but with the meaning of the words enacted.

The error of substituting *author's intention for meaning of language* is that it ignores the fact that a written work once created acquires a meaning which, though dependent on men's usage, is still independent of its creator's motives; and interpretation is precisely a search for this meaning. Juristic considerations reinforce these points. Legal norms are laid down for the community, and the members of the community generally cannot be expected to be privy to the legislator's intentions, except so far as the words used convey these. A fortiori, succeeding generations, to whom the statute may apply can only reasonably be held bound by the meaning of its words *to them*. To hold them to some pristine "will" or "intention" of the legislator, even if this were possible, would be a pervasive and recurrent inequity, requiring citizens to understand language addressed to them in some meaning which it may not convey. Indeed, such considerations might ground a persuasive argument that, even if it were correct here to search for the author's intentions, this author — the author-legislator — must reasonably have intended that his language should bind according to the community's understanding of it for the time being, rather than some original understanding of his own. This is surely the deep basis of the judicial stress on the *ordinary* meaning of words when this does not lead to absurdity and the like; it also suggests that this ordinary meaning is to be sought in the usage and social situation of the generation in which the question now arises.[41]

In these circumstances a good deal of the invocation of the legislator's "will" or "intention" must be regarded as fictional or ritual, concealing the unavoidable creative choices which interpretation in a case of any difficulty must involve. The wise codifier may recognize from the start that his work will have to be completed by successive generations.[42] And, whether or not the role of semantic change in these later creative tasks be thus recognized from the start, legal history confirms it as an important fact.[43] The adaptation of the Roman law to the needs of modern European communities was performed by successive ages of glossators, commentators, humanists, and Pandectists who necessarily read the accumulation of the written Roman law with presuppositions, and also with meanings (references and referents), of their own time and society, and not with those of any ancient Roman legislator. This is precisely what Gény and Duguit showed that French courts had done with the Code Napoléon, despite their theoretical stress on the legislator's will. These are legal examples of the reality and importance of the principle of semantic changefulness of meaning, as well as of the thesis that since language is purposive, the purposes of men for the time being which necessitate the recording and transmission of information help to mould the directions of language change.[44] Conversely, they suggest, the attempt to fix responsibility for the interpretation adopted on the "will" or "intention" of the legislator would be an unhelpful course, even if it were possible to take it. For its effect would be to abort essential creative tasks of adapting law to changing conditions. In fact, courts perform these tasks, more or less, and more or less well, whatever the theory of interpretation they purport to follow.

The present writer has explained elsewhere, in terms of the role and limits of syllogistic and other kinds of reasoning, how the system of precedent "can give an appearance of stability and continuity and yet permit constant change." [45] Parts of this explanation lie in the prominence in judicial discourse of various illusory categories, notably the vague or indeterminate categories and sets of competing categories, often operating within the notion of the *ratio decidendi* itself. This explanation is supported and enriched when we view appellate judgments in the present light as discourse of which the meaning is sought. From this semantic standpoint, indeed, it becomes immediately clear that to assume that there can be only one correct *ratio decidendi* of a case, and that such one *ratio* is discoverable, is to assume that a judicial discourse can have only one meaning, and that we can discover this once and for all. [46]

Yet since a judgment is a discourse, finding its meaning must involve ordinary semantic operations. For all categories of language are subject to semantic principles, scientific language, for example, as well as poetic language, [47] and ordinary language as well as legal language. Lawyers do use technical terms, such as "felony," "fee simple," or "mayhem," of closely restricted traditional meaning; but the general truth, and its instant importance, remain. For, as compared with ordinary language, the incidence of such terms of strictly technical usage in judicial discourse is negligible. The grist to the mill of judgments, and judgments themselves, consists mainly of ordinary vernacular language. It is not merely that lay testimony and documents are part of this grist; it is rather that the linguistic frame of all judgments even when they involve the most technical questions, is still ordinary language.

Under a precedent system, moreover, the instant judgment embraces within its meaning the meaning *for the instant purpose* of the often great number of precedent cases, the judgment in each of which also consists of discourse, similarly related to that of earlier cases. In short the instant judgment is, semantically speaking, an attempt to use the symbolizing functions of language to apprehend and characterize a total series of events including the relevant prior judgments, and occurring over a considerable period of time. What unity the series has hangs (as it were) on the court's present view of the issue in the instant case, and on its interpretation of the meaning of each earlier case. Each judgment, furthermore, is itself made up of smaller symbolic units, and this whole complex symbolization is directed to deciding the competing claims of fact and law in the instant case, in order to determine whether and how the given body of legal controls will be brought to bear. The purposive nature of language and the complex of symbols constituting it, are thus deeply involved. The *ratio decidendi* of the instant judgment (if there is *one* such) must stand in some relation to the referent, it must be some kind of semantic reflection of this whole complex of symbols used in the instant judgment. Neither the *ratio* nor this referent is perceptible by the senses. Nor can we ever hope, as we can with a single symbol for an abstraction such as "justice," to find any *single* referent for this *complex* of symbols by resort to traditional usage, and contextual containment.

The judgment then is a complex purposive unit of discourse symbolically apprehending certain factual situations, as well as prior judicial discourses selected by reference to the socio-emotive purpose of the judge in the context of the instant case as he sees it. The implications of this complex situation are of the greatest concern. It would obviously be a semantic miracle if any *one* meaning of such a discourse-complex should present itself as the *only* correct meaning to all those who read it. In this semantic perspective, indeed, it is difficult even to see what can be meant by searching for *the (one) ratio decidendi* of the instant case. To expect to find such a single *ratio* is to assume that what is usually a vast complex of discourse can have *only one* meaning. It is a gross repudiation of the semantic insight that whether we are concerned with a word, or a judgment, or a whole book, the principles of plurisignation and semantic change operate.

All this, of course, is not to say that the complex of discourse which is a judgment has no meaning, or is indiscriminately variable in meaning. To reject the fantasy of one correct determinate meaning (and therefore one possible *ratio*), is not to accept the opposite fantasy that choice of meaning (and therefore *ratio*) is always at large. The area of meaning of each word is somewhat de-limited syntactically in its sentence, and is further restricted by the contextual environment of each sentence, and the whole complex of discourse by a range of issues any of which the court may re-gard as the *issue* in the case, and by the social situation within which the issues arise. These relations give purpose and direction, and therefore *some delimitation* of the area of meaning, but *no one necessarily correct* determinate meaning, to the entire judgment.

When this complex of judicial discourse is sought to be used by a later court as a precedent for that court's instant decision, the dif-ferent issues in the later social situation may widen the possible area of meaning of the earlier judicial discourse. The continuing openness of old decisions to reinterpretation of their supposed "single *ratio*" *aliis intuitis* in successive generations with different social experience, is commonplace to the thoughtful lawyer. T. C. Pollock has pointed out, in relation to literature,[48] that the author organizes verbal stimuli to control the reader's response, the words of his discourse being conditional stimuli, so that literature is "the utterance of a series of symbols capable of invoking in the mind of the reader a controlled experience."[49] But he has nevertheless to recognize that these stimuli evoke different experiences in different readers. It is with judgments as it is with literature,[50] that no one single experience or understanding of them is necessarily, or even usually, transmitted. From the very nature of the notion of the pre-scriptive *ratio decidendi*, we have elsewhere shown, possibilities for choice surround *ab initio* the *ratio* attributable to a single case, and may continue to arise and even increase as later judgments cluster around it. Choice within the leeways also obviously imports creative activity.[51] It is well to point out, even now, that this truth, there based on logical grounds, has also a concurrent semantic basis.

We need finally to remind ourselves that the plurisignation which thus continuously presents openings for creative choice in precedent law, affects not only the very language of the ear-lier cases from which later courts have drawn a prescriptive *ratio decidendi,* but also other language in the earlier judgments. That other language has seemed inert hitherto, but its inertness is of the field that lies fallow, which may still spring to life at the hand of a cultivator whose experience and purposes lead him to it. And since most judgments used as precedents are generous of language, it becomes all the more misleading to think that a course of decision always progressively narrows the precise meaning of any one isolable proposition. Precedent law, due to the plurisignation of words (embracing also semantic change in time), may constantly return to *the meaning of the total discourse* of each precedent judgment, as well as of some part of the whole of the even more complex unit of discourse made up of the whole series of judgments chosen by the present judge as bearing on the instant issues as he sees them — that is, as understood for his instant purposes.

In summary, then, a judgment is expressed in language, and whatever be the method of seeking "the *ratio decidendi* of a case," it must take account of the meaning of the judgment *as discourse.* The search for the *ratio* thus becomes subject to semantic problems which render quite illusory the assumption that there is only one possible correct meaning. For these problems make it certain that the discourse will bear many possible meanings; it would be a most extraordinary coincidence if these many possible meanings of each judgment were always reflected in only one correct *ratio decidendi.*

These semantic aspects of the *ratio decidendi* problem, when joined with the logical aspects already covered, have a particular bearing for lawyers at the present time, when experiments are proceeding in the use of electronic computers as aids to legal memory, analysis, and thought.

If there were reason to believe that there is but one *ratio* for each case, verifiable in some way which entitles us to call it *the correct ratio* of that case, we might hope in time to use computers to extract *this correct ratio* once and for all from each important case, machines having already mastered many remarkable tasks of translation of language, as well as the most elaborate tasks of logic and mathematics. The present study, however, of both the logical and semantic aspects of appellate decision-making, makes it clear why at this level of ambition such hopes are quite chimerical. For, quite on the contrary, it affords ample reasons to believe that appellate judgments do *not* usually have only *one* verifiably correct *ratio*; and even the most ingenious machine cannot find what is not there. And while machines could no doubt expose the full range of competing alternative *rationes*, we shall see that in a case of any stature this range is generally too vast to make the exposure useful. We have elsewhere shown this to be so in logic, and the present semantic aspect confirms the conclusion. For there is involved in "the *ratio*" of such a case the meaning of some parts or others of the whole judicial discourse, embracing but transcending any individual word or sentence of the instant judgment; as well as some parts or others of all those precedent judgments on which it builds. No doubt the range of alternative *rationes* could be exposed by the machine, but this range would usually be too large to *control* judgment. It is the emotive components of experience, will, and purpose of human judges which narrow their choices to practicable dimensions. Machines cannot be equipped with these components.

Even if we were to entertain that view of the *ratio* according to which it is determined by the "material" or "important" facts in relation to the decision,[52] the role of the machine would be a very limited one. Let it be supposed too (surely with even more fantastic hazard) that we *could* trust the machine to detect all synonyms in both words and their overtones of the adjectives "material" and "important," and to identify all the facts characterized in the judgment. We would still be far from success. For this view of the *ratio* has to be applied even when the precedent judge may not have explicitly mentioned any facts, nor characterized them by any synonym of "material"; on Professor Goodhart's view, for example, the "material facts" must still be gathered from the whole judicial discourse. We are back then at the main logical and semantic difficulties. This would be so even if we could take at its face value the supposed "objectivity" of the process of identifying the "material facts." We have shown, however, that this claim to objectivity is un-justified, and that the finding of "materiality" is in part an emotive judgment of the fitness of the earlier decision for present purposes. We return again to the deeper reason for the limits on the machine; for it cannot be equipped to make such an *emotive* judgment be-fore scanning the material which it stores.

It is true that the contrast of emotive and scientific discourse is not now so central in semantic thought as it was in Ogden and Richards' *Meaning of Meaning* in 1923.[53] Yet the fact that language has an emotive function still cannot be dismissed.[54] Lan-guage is sometimes used emotively, and the characterization of some facts in a case as the "material" ones is without doubt very often "emotive" or "affective" in function. In cases whose *ratio* is still being searched for, this "emotive" or "affective" element is at-tributable to the experience, purpose, and will of the judges con-cerned, and may not correspond to any objective features of the language used for which a machine could scan.[55]

It might indeed be disastrous for the growth of law, as an instru-ment responsible to men's changing experience and convictions from age to age, if a machine *could* also scan for the emotive or affective elements of judgment. For, if the precedent system (*stare decisis*) then continued to work at all, all later generations would remain harnessed to the experience and convictions of their more or less remote ancestors. But changing experience and convictions, not to speak of the changing environment, are at the heart of both the growth and the stable viability of precedent law. Machines which brought them, too, into a calculus of binding *rationes* would strike at that heart. We shall elaborate some of these practical con-sequences of the semantic frame of judicial discourse in the exam-ination of recent behavioralist work, and the potentialities of com-puters for legal tasks, to which we now turn.

This view of the potentialities of machines as a means of extract-ing "the *ratio decidendi*" of a case, does not deny their other more modest but still important potentialities.[56] These, however, are mainly in the nature of document or information retrieval; and they are useful primarily for data already sufficiently precise in their symbolization, and sufficiently free of affective elements.[57] An experimental machine at the Law Center of the University of Pittsburgh has made almost instantaneously available by storage on magnetic tapes access to the contents of American statutes on health, of all Pennsylvania statutes, and a fifth of those of each of ten other states and of the United States. The United States Patent Office performs important parts of its specialized legal tasks with computers. Experiments with the more difficult task of retrieving the data of case law are proceeding, for instance, in the Southwest legal foundation at Southern Methodist University.[58] Reports on key-words of cases on particular matters, such as oil, have been analyzed, coded, and stored in machines which are programed to allow retrieval of requested combinations of the data.

The 235 volumes of the American Digest System from 1916 to 1961 comprise 7¾ million digest paragraphs. The American State, Federal and National Reporter volumes for the same period covered 10,409 volumes. The addition of 11,650 pre-1916 volumes gives a grand total of 22,058 volumes of reports of cases since 1789. This mass continues to mount in far more than annual proportion. In 1958 alone, American state and federal courts were authors of not less than 108,000 pages comprising 76½ million words. Chief Justice Vanderbilt calculated that in 1953 there were 2,100,000 reported American decisions, compared with 5,000 English cases in Coke's time, and 10,000 in Mansfield and Blackstone's time. He estimated that the state and federal statutes passed in 1952–1953 numbered 29,938, supplementing the past accumulation of 931 volumes. Administrative regulations accessible in the Code of 1949 were 41 volumes of 22,055 pages. The current Federal Register in 1954 comprised 9,910 pages. There have to be added of course the vast volumes of reports of cases in administrative agencies, such as the Tax Court, Interstate Commerce Commission, Labor Relations Board, and Bureau of Internal Revenue. The English position, though not so impossible, is still menacing enough. The count of British law reports as long ago as 1916 was 6,836 volumes. In 1963, it has been pointed out, England alone counts over 100 current series of law reports and legal periodicals and that altogether any of nearly 2,000 different series of reports, some comprising more than 100 volumes each, may become relevant in a search on the law.[59]

In these circumstances we must obviously not underrate the importance of machines for the humbler tasks of retrieval. Even here, however, we must attend to dangers and obstacles, of which only one or two can be mentioned. One great danger arises from the fact that the discourse of judges must first be stabilized, sterilized, and otherwise reduced to permit it to be stored in the machines. Insofar as lawyers then work with what the machine feeds back rather than using its output as a mere guide to the original judicial discourse, many mobile, living, emotive, and literary elements on which the growth of the law in part depends may be cut off. This danger is aggravated, moreover, by the very superiority of machine retrieval over traditional techniques. For it is already clear from the course of experimentation that the vast increase in relevant data which the machines may thrust before the lawyer is such as to increase the temptation of lawyers and judges to decide matters on the understanding of those who fix input and program for machines, more than on that of earlier judges. It may be that the mass of machine output may be reduced by using more stringent standards of relevance in input and programing generally. This, however, has other dangers of arbitrary exclusion of what in later circumstances might become deeply relevant. In the search for a balance that is both useful and feasible we must still finally depend on the learning, penetration, and insights of the unmechanized human mind; nor, as we understand them, are the responsible champions of computers for the most part unaware of this.

III

IT SEEMS to be acknowledged, on all hands, though sometimes grudgingly, that the recent concern of behavioral scientists [60] with legal and (especially) judicial decision-making continues, with better work-plans and instruments, a main line of "legal realist" challenge of the 'twenties and 'thirties. They seek, as the realists had done, more adequate bases for understanding judicial decisions than the apparent operative meaning of the words in which courts have purported to embody it.[61] Like them, therefore, they begin by discounting legal propositions as formulated in opinions. Like them they insist that other determining factors in decision-making must be found, and seek to interpret past decisions in terms of a range of factors which would allow better understanding and prediction.

The contemporary movement is, however, also very different. First, its central drive is to identify the operative factors in forms that are measurable, so as to allow a quantitative analysis of judicial behavior.[62] Schubert has here resorted to complementary methods of "bloc-analysis" and "scalogram" analysis. The former is designed to detect regularities in concurrence and conflict of decisions among members of a collegiate court, the latter aims to measure attitudes of judges towards specific policy issues in the course of decision.[63] Second, of course, the present movement has available vastly more efficient and refined techniques and instruments of measurement and computation. Third, it is an important difference that their work is inspired mainly from the area of political science. On the one hand, their lack of lawyers' traditionalism encourages boldness in hypothesis, and may even reduce tendentious and polemical drives. "Outsiders" may be more indulged than "rebels." On the other hand, lack of depth of knowledge of legal processes and the traditional body of juristic thought makes the risk of error and naïveté substantial. Fourth, as to their achievements, behavioralists are claiming on the basis of their more precise methods to predict future decisions of individual judges with substantial certainty, even in such notoriously difficult areas as due process and civil rights. If they are right they have turned legal realist aspiration into behavioralist performance. Nor is it necessary for us here to take a position as to the degree of certainty with which newly applied techniques of multivariate factor analysis, the scalogram, bloc-analysis, and model-building and digital computers,[64] with or without built-in memory or forgetfulness, will in fact allow reliable prediction of the future decisions of individual judges. For present purposes it will suffice to assume that the most sanguine hopes of reducing the margin of error will be realized.[65]

It is clear that, even prediction apart, the new techniques and tools must eventually aid in many ways towards lawyers' handling of the intractable masses of authoritative materials of the law. If we mention only some examples of such services, it is because we are attempting not a stocktaking of what is clear, but rather to focus on one debatable area against a sufficient background to permit interdisciplinary communication concerning it. For this it suffices to illustrate rather than exhaust the background matters.

First, then, there is the most indubitable service of the computer itself, already well begun, of storing in various alternative forms the flood of past and current legal materials, so as to permit instant retrieval under skilled programing of what is relevant to the particular business. Even apart from impending improvements in *information* retrieval, the mere retrieval of documents such as headnotes of cases, or parts, or summaries or the whole of judgments, statutes, or legal literature generally is likely to afford savings in search time which are incalculable. Few lawyers would gainsay its importance, in relation to which we ourselves would perhaps be disposed not to overstress here the caveats we raised in section II as to the importance of what the machines might lose of the emotive components of judicial discourse during storage and retrieval. For the critical dangers of this are mainly in what we here call the judgment of justice, a matter we approach in any case separately. Second, besides such legal materials, machines would give lawyers access to vast and complex bodies of non-legal knowledge hitherto virtually not accessible to them at all. American legal practice ranges more than that in most other countries over subjects like antitrust law, tax law, public utilities, labor, planning, and public law, calling for reference to non-legal areas like economics, accounting, statistics, transportation and communications, labor relations, criminology, psychology. Here machine techniques of central storage and retrieval may not only save time, but often make lawyer's access possible at all, and perhaps also mitigate by their objectivity the chronic evils now associated with reliance on mostly partisan expert personnel. For while such personnel could obviously not be wholly replaced, these could, up to a point, be a nonpartisan check on them, reducing the area of the less responsible partisanship.[66] Services in the nature of retrieval of data of all kinds seem to be unqualified in the boons they promise to confer on all levels of legal officials, from lawyers advising clients to all levels of courts themselves. The time saved and greater efficiency of search are of great importance to all of them.

Prediction of decision itself, though its mention quickly raises polemical fire, holds promise of relief from some of the undoubted ills of American law and justice, like congestion, backlog, and delays in the courts. Reliable prediction of future appellate holdings [67] could, in the hands of lawyers advising clients, encourage both lawyers and clients to settle many claims without thrusting excessive personal responsibility on the advising lawyer, and with substantial gains in time and efficiency for courts and litigants generally. Such techniques of tolerably accurate prediction of appellate holdings as to the applicable law could also be said to promise much help to lower courts, without serious countervailing risks. Decisions as to what is the law at these levels rarely determine the ongoing movement of the legal order. And as to justice for the particular litigants, assuming the margin of predictive error to be small, only a small proportion of litigants would be prejudicially affected. These would still have, of course, the right to appeal; and under the conditions prevailing in many inferior courts, it is likely that the number of those prejudicially affected by bad guessing on the law is already no less serious. Nor need these new techniques of search for the law worsen the lawyer's image at this level. Even when they needed to be obtruded in face of laymen, they would probably seem no more mysterious and incomprehensible to him than ordinary legal operations already often are. So that the economics of time from the new predictive techniques, the checks on corruption and inefficiency which they might provide at the lower court level, and the question of their use at that level, must at least be left open.[68]

IV

THIS LEVEL of use of predictive techniques by lower courts to help them form a view of how appellate courts would determine a point of law, now involved in the lower court's decision, must be seen as occupying a critical borderline position.[69] The aim of this essay is to identify this border, to characterize the differences between the universes of thought which it separates, and to invite earnest dialogue concerning it between legal scholars and behavioral scientists. These distinct universes of thought (we believe) are on the one side, that of an observer's prediction of how an appellate judge will decide an instant case before it and, on the other, that of the appellate judge's own act of judgment as he has to make it from the judgment seat.

It is clear enough that for the most part the jurist, the political scientist, and even the lawyer advising his client or preparing for hearing, are in the position of observers. For the trial lawyer the future behavior of the hearing judge and of appellate judges who might be involved is properly examinable by such predictive techniques as there are. Experienced trial lawyers have always regarded this as part of preparing for trial, sometimes to the point of trying to arrange for trial before a judge from whom the predicted result is more favorable. Moreover, as regards certain elements in his decision, even the trial judge himself, despite the fact that he is deciding this case, may also be in the position of an observer. In particular, so far as there are doubts as to where the appellate courts stand with regard to the rule applicable to the case, the trial judge is necessarily involved in prediction, not indeed of his own instant decision, but of what the appellate courts *will decide* in this type of case. And it is only and essentially here that we have left open the propriety (and net gain in efficiency) from use even by lower court judges of new and sufficiently reliable techniques of prediction.

By the same token, however, when the appellate judge confronts the duty of making *his* authoritative decision as to this applicable rule of law, usually at a point in the judicial hierarchy which spells judicial finality, we are *at the other side of our critical border*; and this for three main reasons. One is that the decision now to be made by him is likely *ex hypothesi* to be beyond the limits of hitherto finally settled law, so that it does not merely declare what the existing law is, but rather decides what justice requires that the law should be. (We include tacitly here, to avoid complicating the argument, the case of reversal of earlier decisions, that is, of creative decisions which *unsettle* and *resettle* law: for this is a fortiori creative.) It is this kind of creative judgment that we here term a "judgment of justice"; it is a *creative* judicial act. A second reason is that this kind of judgment is creative *of law*, and that it is now a commonplace of juristic thought that due stability and due movement of advanced legal orders both depend upon adequate regular performance of such creative judicial acts. A third reason (valid, we would suppose, for all who reject the natural-law claim that an inexhaustible store of just legal principles lies always ready for discovery by reason) is that these creative acts involve something additional to the perceptive and cognitive and conceptualizing faculties. Whether we think of this something more in terms of acts of will, or choice or preference, they are acts which the judge must be allowed and encouraged to perform with integrity on the basis of such experience, insight, and emotion as it has been given him to acquire *up to the very moment of performance*.

V

WHEN I SPEAK of this area where an appellate judge must render a judgment of justice I am of course speaking of his choice of values to be realized in law. And though I have ventured to think in section II above that the leading behavioralists in this area are not really concerned with the judgment of justice, I do not of course assume that in their search for reliable methods of predicting judicial behavior they are unaware that their data consists of past judgments of justice. On the contrary, it is pre-eminently this area of judicial activity which has most provoked and inspired them. Glendon Schubert's *Quantitative Analysis of Judicial Behavior* in 1959 focused on classes of decision in the Supreme Court of the United States where the indeterminacies of the constitutional instrument and changing social situations have thrown up new problem after new problem involving value-choices and their effectuation through law. By the same token it has been in decisions about which the Justices have tended to divide in either their holdings or reasons, and where since the merits of the various standpoints were problematical in terms of existing legal propositions, that attempts at explanation are forced beyond these propositions to the search for non-legal factors to serve as the determining variables. It is above all these non-legal variables which the behavioralists have set out to identify, delimit, and describe in quantitative terms. Their bloc-analysis concerns itself with variables consisting of relations of stable or changing influence between members of the court; the scalogram analysis with variables consisting of value-attitudes of each judge. Explanation is then sought for decisions of each judge, in terms of the degree of presence (in a quantitative sense) of each of the identified variables — by a multivariate analysis in this sense. Insofar as this shows a degree of concurrence of given variables with given kinds of decisions not explicable by mere chance, this concurrence may be expected to repeat itself in future decisions. In this way concurrence of given combinations of variable factors with given kinds of past decisions is taken to base prediction of future decisions. Conversely the degree of accuracy of such predictions is taken to constitute a kind of experimental verification of the adequacy of the factor identification and quantitation of prediction.

Values held by the sitting judge are of course among the range of factors considered by behavioralists, and they have indeed offered ambitious schematizations of "recorded notions of justice and social utility, and various natural and social factors, as operative through and by interaction between various policy makers, policy appliers and policy recipients." [70] The informed lawyer will admire the aspirations to system and precision in the elaborate check-lists thus afforded, even when he suspects that they contain little (save the claim to systematize and measure) which has not already long been recognized in the best juristic thinking about judicial decision-making.[71] He will perhaps also wonder about the predictive power which can really emerge from attempts to work with such disparate variables, some of them vastly oversimplified in formulation.[72] But however this be, it seems clear that the study of the values held by each judge as manifest both on and off the bench is tending to become quite central in attempted prediction of future decisions, along with other variables of perception, personality, leadership, and role within the going multi-judge group, as well as *vis-à-vis* other selected groups or individuals clustered around this. Here too, hypotheses are sought which are "quantitatively" verifiable by accurate prediction of each justice's votes in universes of cases not used in developing the hypotheses.[73]

Somewhat parenthetically to the present purpose we may offer certain observations concerning any design to rely exclusively on quantifiable non-legal values-as-held as a basis of explanation and prediction. One is that this design would have to exclude the type of case that may still arise even on the appellate level where a judge's decision is determined by his view of what the law as it stands requires of him. On this basis his vote might go against all the non-legal values which he sincerely holds.[74] Second, it is a juristic commonplace that judicial solutions often proceed by the compromises between several conflicting "values" rather than clean preference of some to others. Even if some objective quantification of each value-variable is conceivable, it seems difficult to conceive of an objective way of quantifying the degrees of frustration or realization in the complex of values operating on the single judicial vote. Third, and perhaps most serious, even the quantification of single values may present mysteries bringing the objectivity of quantified rendering into doubt. After all, the meaning of some of them has engaged philosophers for thousands of years, "pleasure," "liberty," and "the public good" not least among them. Fourth, if we try to proceed on the basis of the judge's own held values as manifest in his past decisions and statements we must be constantly alert to the impact on him now in isolation of values prevalent in the community, and of factual social data à la Brandeis brief,[75] as the judge may *now* perceive and receive them. Present judgment may be deeply influenced by such community values and factual data newly perceived or received from time to time, as well as by the judge's held values as manifest in his past decisions and statements. And finally, as already briefly indicated, when behavioralists seek to take into account a sufficiently wide range of elements, the question becomes whether all these can be given a form susceptible of measurement by genuinely objective methods. Some questions on this very point are raised by political scientists and economists themselves.[76]

For present purposes, however, what is significant about the focus of behavioralists on values held by the judge is that it seems to bring their concerns very close to the problems of decision-making as they appear to the judge in the judgment seat of justice. And this seems at odds with the opinion we expressed above that their stance is essentially that of observers interested in what proceeds *from* judgment, but rather uninterested in any empathic sharing of the agony of making the judgment of justice, or in the feedback of their work on this agony.

But it is only superficially at odds. For even when they take the values held by the judge as factors, behavioralists still are only observers, looking at what has already been done in judgment; when they turn their attention in the course of prediction to future judgments it is not to ask what the judge should do to further justice, but only what kind of decision he will give if he acts consistently with values attributed to him on the basis of his past decisions.

VI

THE CAUSES of anxiety central to this essay arise precisely from this deceptive appearance of behavioralist concern with the judgment of justice when in reality this is not a behavioralist concern. If we could assume that this appearance would never mislead, and that the diversity of objectives would be respected, there would be need, perhaps, neither of anxiety nor of clarifying dialogue.

Even, however, if behavioralists were always clear on this matter, it could not be lightly assumed that their interpreters and followers would see and respect this basic distinction. And wherever it is not respected we face the risks of substituting mere calculations of factor-associations in past decisions for the search which ought to go on now at the judgment seat for solutions *as just as the judge can now make them.* We already find a leading Japanese legal scholar, after enthusiastically demonstrating the predictive power of scalogram analysis in Japanese civil liberty cases, concluding euphorically: "if this line of inquiry advances, the day might come . . . when we lawyers also shall use an electronic machine in predicting judicial behaviour, and when the *courts will use one in arriving at their decisions — a new version of the slot machine theory not necessarily unimaginable, or 'mechanical jurisprudence' in the literal sense of the term."* [77] The fact that even on his sanguine account there is a Schubertian-acknowledged ten-per-cent margin of error [78] seems unimportant to this learned writer.

Yet, as we venture again to stress, we are concerned in the Japanese Supreme Court, as in that of the United States, with the area of the appellate judge's present judgment of justice where both lawyers and behavioralists should be aware that reliance at the judgment seat on new predictive techniques for positive guidance would seriously threaten the judge's central concern with justice itself. For if the results thus predicted for him do affirmatively guide him in present decision, as distinct from merely warning him of any pattern of caprice or adventitious bias in his earlier decisions, each judge will tend to vote somewhat more steadily in accordance with what is predicted for him. The former margin of deviant instances would accordingly tend to disappear in deference to predicted patterns, aided by the human tendency to follow the less agonizing because already trodden path. Nor can we wholly dismiss such dangers merely in terms of unlikelihood that a judge will resort for counsel to predictions of his own behavior. For a certain feedback and Heisenberg effect of prediction on future decisions seems unavoidable in any case.

The first ill effect of this would be to reduce the earnestness of review of past holdings, related as this is to judicial vacillation, afterthought, awareness of new implications and social settings, and to the sparking clash of dissent. I here plead, therefore, for a common juristic and behavioralist recognition of the historical importance of legal change springing from deviance, tentativeness, and even indecision in judgment, resulting in sensitiveness to new ideas or newly perceived social situations and indeed, often, to Hamlet-like introspection and vacillation. For here lie some of the main ways of growth of that social good which we call "justice."

Second, behind this effect, but also probably independent of it, is the ill effect on judgment of the very notion that a judge searching for a just solution might use some routinized means based on the past to predict what he will (or should) find to be just, rather than to *decide now* as best he can *what is just for the future*. And this point is so central that I must try to state it without equivocation or evasion, a task by no means easy.

It has long been a juristic commonplace that even the best designed, elaborated, and formulated body of precepts will constantly fall short of giving clear answers, or will come to give unacceptable answers, as new situations arise for their application. In the judicial process, as the precursors and pioneers of sociological jurisprudence showed, the area of falling short includes the area which demands judicial judgments of justice. Results in this area do not depend merely on intellectual operations with the existing body of precepts, though (whether empirical or mathematical-logical) these are of course involved and need to be well done. Results also depend on emotive reactions, evaluations, and preferences. They are a product of heart as well as mind, of unanalyzed and even unintellectualized experience of present living, as well as of the analyzed and intellectualized account, ranging from history to myth, of men's past activities. In due course, no doubt, the present act of doing justice will, in its turn, be reduced to intellectualized forms which can be processed independently of nonintellectual elements. But not so with the *present* act of judgment or (we should rather say) with the judgment *still to be made here in the present.*

This at the outset. But my own work of twenty years ago [79] showed that it is largely those aspects of precedent doctrine which are enshrouded in chronically intractable problems of an analytical-logical nature, which provide the room and set the scene for regular entry of considerations of justice upon the judgment scene. It is precisely here, where we cannot intellectually lay out and control the decisional trends in advance, that there often emerge those acts of judgment which give the movement and direction to the legal order which make this a means towards justice as men are given to understand it. Here too, as we *retrospect* upon past direction and movement the outcome may be rationalized in terms of empirical data and logical relations; and from them, with or without the aid of machines, we may be able to "explain" past decisions and even predict future ones. This, however, is only up to a certain point and on certain assumptions; and where this point will be, and how long these assumptions will be valid, are still subject to future intellectually intractable events of the kind involved in judgments of justice. What may be "adequate" truth in terms of retrospect on past decisions, may still not be the important part of *what is still to be done from the judgment seat.*

Among the vital processes occurring at these intellectually intractable points of precedent growth are the modification, supplementation, or even abandonment of reigning legal precepts by reference to the contemporary social situations, ideas, and ideals. It is because the doctrine of precedent, as many lawyers as well as social scientists still misunderstand it, does not allow for the operation of these processes, that their occurrence is an ever-continuing source of trauma. Nor is it surprising that the agent of these processes should be *the man* in the appellate judgment seat, endowed as he usually is by the very contemporaneity of his life experience with the temper, perplexities, insights, and preferences of men of his own community. And when we ask how he is able to fill this role it is certainly not by giving judgments which conform to prediction based on *past* performances, but rather by choosing and willing a decision which is *now* just in his eyes. This is at least part of the reason why he plays a Trojan-horse-like role against existing legal precepts, but he does so in the name of the ongoing legal order, and the justice which it should realize. And it is also why this role is so difficult to articulate in cogent intellectual terms. Whether we look to moving prose and poetic insights and paradoxes à la Cardozo, to antinomies à la Radbruch or Pound, to the caution-valor game à la Pollock or to the alternating laudations and pejoratives about particular decisions otherwise barely distinguished, à la Llewellyn, all such attempted articulations have remained, so far as the intellect is concerned, ambivalent or indeterminate.[80] Men in their search to do justice seem always to be transcending the drive, methods, and limits of mere intellect. So that insofar as we delegate *this particular search* to machines, even by inadvertence, we shall risk its emasculation to the level of the incapacity of machines to do what cannot be intellectualized.

It is at this point above all that we must listen to the *non possumus* of the machine. Traditionalist objections to various other uses of machine techniques may, as we have seen, be misguided in relation to the future fuller potentialities of machines. For instance, while thus far machines tend by their very efficiency to retrieve so many relevant authorities that we may lose as much in time from the need of further manual selection and evaluation as we save by the initial search, this can probably be controlled by more selective programing and requests. If we think that the casual ignoring of precedents is one of the advantages of lawyers' traditional manual techniques, we may be able to build forgetfulness and oversight into machine programs. And it is at any rate on the horizon that machines may be made which will not only retrieve stored data, but will remember and learn from what they store and retrieve, making their output still more selective and limited.[81]

This potentiality cannot however override the *non possumus* of computer techniques when confronted by the mission of doing justice. "The computers," one of the staunchest supporters of their use by lawyers has observed, "have just one inescapable theoretical limitation; every term and operation must be made explicit and nothing can be presumed, assumed, implied, or based on intuition." [82] And this a fortiori means that machines cannot *will* to do justice as men can do and judges are required to try to do. It would not suffice to this end to build into machines the capacity to forget or to overlook, which human judges constantly display. For this capacity, like logic and the neglect of it, is not the substance of the task of doing justice; when relevant it is but an outward sign that the activity of seeking justice may be proceeding in the domain of will and choice. And the quality of justice done finally depends, not on any incidental forgetting or overlooking as such, but on the will exercised and the choice made by the man in the judgment seat.

Another way of saying this is that the forgetting and overlooking that may enter into the appellate doing of justice are not random but may represent a selection arising from men's striving with heart as well as head. It is selection, moreover, which cannot be tied to average past performances and therefore extrapolated.[83] It has rather to be made by the individual man in his uniqueness, and in the uniqueness (for him) of each moment of judgment, "with all his heart, and with all his soul and with all his might." No doubt this still leaves mystery at the central point of the judgment of justice, and (which is the same thing) leaves it enshrouded often in problematical and even misleading intellectualized disguises.[84] If we fix our minds on the social role of these superficialities of disguise, we have to ask with Hans Baade [85] whether in the light of widespread deadlock, ineptitude, and inertia in legislatures, on the one hand, and popular hostility to judicial law-making on the other, the legal order can dispense with all the intellectualized trappings which accompany it. But the heart of the matter, we here insist, lies not in the trappings but in what goes on beneath.[86]

To be carelessly oversanguine, as some may tend to become in envisaging the appellate judge arriving at his decision by consulting an electronic machine, is in effect to remove from him the duty of this present striving for justice at each moment of judgment. Justice then would no longer be a man-created value; nor unless machines become God and mathematics His doctrine, would justice then be a God-created value either. To reject both these alternatives would leave little indeed to be said about justice.

VII

I SHOWED at the outset some of the limits set by semantic change, and by the emotive functions of language as well for machine-retrieval of data as for machine-based prediction of judicial decision. I was also concerned to draw attention, these limits notwithstanding, to the many potential services of machines to law and lawyers. These included time-saving methods of retrieval of documents and information, in face of the mounting mass of precedent, statute law, and legal literature, as well as access to great bodies of extra-legal data which may become relevant to particular legal problems. They also included predictions of future appellate holdings as to the law *so far as these may safely come to serve the practitioners advising clients*, relieving grave congestions of legal and litigious business. For we have seen that once a high degree of reliability is reached, conscientious lawyers may well and properly undertake more responsibility in securing settlement of out of court cases. It may also be open to argument (though less clearly, we suggested) that access to such predictions might show a balance of gain over risk *even for lower court judges, when decisions depend on a doubtful point of law still to be clarified at appellate level.*

At this point in the use of machine and behavioralist prediction we pointed to the critical border between service to the legal order and the subversion of it. The possible subversion with which we have been here concerned arises from the duty resting upon appellate judges to fix or change from time to time *the direction of movement of the law* by what we have termed judgments of justice. For, I have said, whenever an appellate judge faces this duty, and has to do justice in this sense, it is his duty to address himself to it *with his own present experience and insights.* It would be a corruption of justice for him to shortcut this duty by resting for positive guidance for present decision on predictions of his future decisions based on his own past behavior; still more so if the basis is the average past behavior of a group of judges.

VIII

JEROME FRANK's demand for complete judicial awareness and articulation of all factors entering into judgment, if we tried to build these into institutional arrangements, would vastly increase the internal and external stresses upon judges.[87] Save with the very ablest this would lead, in day-after-day, year-after-year functioning, to increasing stress, delay, faltering of decision, and even breakdown. And the recruiting of abler men would become progressively more difficult. So that the judicial institution would be threatened both in its incumbents and the succession after them.

The behavioralist approach, if it does not come to understand the limits and dangers discussed in the present paper, would also threaten the judicial institution, but now from the other extreme. It would tend, in the very measure of its success, to dull the appellate judge's awareness of his personal choice and responsibility in setting new or changed directions for legal growth. It would tend to submerge and lose the acts of will and choice which are at this level involved in justice, in an apparently impersonal pattern of past behavior tendencies of this judge, or of a group of judges including him. Insofar as predictions so based tend to influence *this judge* towards the predicted result, we would have a feedback of past decisions which transmutes *past actual behavior* into spurious *present justice.* The judge of justice so influenced would be a self-frustrating judge, dulled to that sense of final human responsibility hitherto found in men's questings after justice.

Appellate judges so supported would no doubt be less prone to weaken and falter than under the strains of intense and constant consciousness of personal choice demanded by Jerome Frank's picture of the ideally just judge. For they would be to a degree metamorphosed into carefree combinations of digits stored in a computer, awaiting an occasional timely retrieval. There is happily still time, before either of these designs matures, for us to reexamine what is needful to keep judicial institutions viable under modern conditions of legislative, documentary, and decisional "explosions," as well as to preserve the beat of *human* justice at the appellate heart of the ongoing legal order.

We believe, on the first head, that juristic traditionalism will have to be more receptive to new techniques than it has yet become if viability of our modern complex legal orders and their institutions is to avoid breakdown. By the same token, however, we believe that the pioneers and experts of the new techniques must face up to the limits of what contributions they can make. This implies on their part a certain caution against stirring false hopes. We need to recognize, for instance, that no system of thought which continues to use language and which lacks the power to arrest the changeful contexts of social life and its emergent problems, can escape the process of semantic change and uncertainty. There is need also for the positive contribution of a common scholarly approach alongside the juristic tradition to the perplexities of justice as wrestled with in the appellate judgment seat,[88] rather than merely as reported at the side lines. Neither lawyers nor behavioral scientists are entitled to leave the judgment seat quite untended while the computers stand ready to process the outcome of its everrenewing struggle for justice through but beyond the law. All of us must acknowledge together in the new age of the machine the simple but deep wisdom of the aphorism of the Father of Cybernetics: "Render unto man what is man's," he said, "and unto the machine only what is the machine's."

Notes

NOTES

Where Law and Social Science Stand

1. See Hermann Kantorowicz, "Savigny and the Historical School of Law" (1937), 53 *Law Quarterly Review* 334, 335. Rudolf von Jhering's *Geist des römischen Rechts auf den verschiedenen Stufen seiner Entwicklung* (1873–77, 4 vols., unfinished) is, in one aspect, such an inquiry directed to "technique" and "ideal" elements in the Roman law.

   Both the category of "historical jurisprudence" and its "comparative" variant have been abandoned by the present writer. See Julius Stone, *The Province and Function of Law* (1946), 35–36 (hereafter cited as *Province*); Julius Stone, *Legal System and Lawyers' Reasonings* (1964), introduction, § 8 (hereafter cited as *Legal System*). F. J. Davis, H. H. Foster, Jr., C. R. Jeffery, and E. E. Davis, *Society and the Law* (1962), 9, 14, and n. 56, are correct to stress this aspect of the present writer's approach. And see the substantive study once this ground is cleared in Julius Stone, *Social Dimensions of Law and Justice* (1966) (hereafter cited as *Social Dimensions*).

2. See n. 57 below and for fuller general bibliographies (1961–62) 10–11 *Current Sociology*, No. 1, with introductory summary article by W. G. Friedmann, and No. 4 in a series of seven monthly supplements, "Frontiers of Legal Research" (1963), 7 *American Behavioral Scientist*, issue coordinator, C. L. Ruttenberg (hereafter cited as "Legal Research"). Friedmann sees "the sociological approach to law" as including "ethnological and anthropological studies" and "psychological and psychoanalytical explanation of law," as well as "the more obviously sociological studies of such writers as Max Weber or Eugen Ehrlich, and the sociologically oriented teleology of law characterised by . . . Ihering and Pound." The articles in "Legal Research" attempt to guide lawyers briefly to relevant aspirations of behavioral scientists, and the Supplement thereto seeks to guide non-lawyers to juristic work relevant for the behavioral scientist. The latter, particularly, should be used with caution as to both inclusions and omissions.

For an attempted thumbnail guide to relevant work in psychology see Charles Winick, "A Primer of Psychological Theories Holding Implications for Legal Work," in "Legal Research," 45–47, and works he cites on p. 47.

3. For reasons just given we shall unless otherwise indicated use such terms as "the study of law in society," "sociological jurisprudence," or "sociology of law" for literary variation without differences in meaning.

4. Kantorowicz, "Savigny and the Historical School of Law," 334; Eugen Ehrlich, *Fundamental Principles of the Sociology of Law* (*Grundlegung der Soziologie des Rechts*, 1913, translated by W. L. Moll, 1936), 478ff. (hereafter cited as *Sociology*); N. S. Timasheff, *An Introduction to the Sociology of Law* (1939), 45ff. (hereafter cited as *Sociology of Law*).

5. R. Saleilles, "Ecole Historique et Droit Naturel d'après Quelques Ouvrages Récents" (1902), 1 *Revue Trimestrielle de Droit Civil* 80 (hereafter cited as "Ecole Historique").

6. See Julius Stone, review of J. W. Hurst, *Law and Economic Growth* (1964), in (1965), 78 *Harvard Law Review* 1687–1689.

7. See for various accounts in relation to law: Timasheff, *Sociology of Law*, 44–63 (brief but with a comprehensive but occasionally uneven bibliography at 381–403); Georges Gurvitch, *Sociology of Law* (1942), 68–197 (the fullest chronological account in English, though the author is rather impatient with ideas inconsistent with his own); Huntington Cairns, *Law and the Social Sciences* (1935) (hereafter cited as *Social Sciences*); Ehrlich, *Sociology*, Ch. i.

8. See Julius Stone, *Human Law and Human Justice* (1965), Ch. 4 (hereafter cited as *Human Justice*).

9. Cf. Cairns, *Social Sciences*, 132–133.

10. See for general accounts Stone, *Province*, Ch. 9; Stone, *Human Justice*, Chs. 1–2, and 7.

11. See Eugen Ehrlich, "Montesquieu and Sociological Jurisprudence" (1916), 29 *Harvard Law Review* 582.

12. See especially Stone, *Social Dimensions*, Chs. 2–3, 10ff.

13. There are several English translations. Comte's *Cours de Philosophie Positive* appeared much earlier, 1830–42.

14. Cairns, *Social Sciences*, and cf. the same author's *The Theory of Legal Science* (1941), 50ff. The fact that Leibnitz in the seventeenth and Comte in the nineteenth century both used a mathematical model seems, however, a hazardous basis for saying with Cairns that "the jurists of the seventeenth century are to be regarded as mechanical sociological jurists equally with those of the middle of the nineteenth century." Leibnitz influenced John Austin as well (see e.g., Vol. 2, *Lectures on Jurisprudence* (2 vols., 3rd edition, revised and edited by Robert Campbell, 1869), 1123), but that scarcely makes Austin a "mechanistic sociological jurist."

15. I.e., the factual meaning of "law" and "order" with the normative meaning. Cairns's main criticism (*Theory of Legal Science*), proceeding on his specification of "disorder" as the prime concept of social science jurisprudence, seems (for reasons more fully examined in Stone, *Province*, Ch. 17) misplaced.

16. E.g., J. B. Lamarck, and T. R. Malthus.
17. The idea of social evolution had been mooted by Herbert Spencer before Darwin in *Social Statics* (1850) and *The Principles of Psychology* (1855) and made quite explicit in Spencer's law of "the survival of the fittest" in "Progress: Its Law and Cause," in Vol. 1 of *Essays: Scientific, Political, Speculative,* 3 vols. (1858–74). The three volumes of the summatory *Principles of Sociology* were published 1880–96. See Stone, *Social Dimensions,* Ch. 9, § 23; and on Spencer's links with the Malthus-Darwin evolution of "evolution" and his influence see A. L. Harding, "The Ghost of Herbert Spencer: A Darwinian Concept of Law," in R. N. Wilkin, J. S. Marshall, T. E. Davitt, and A. L. Harding, *Origins of the Natural Law Tradition* (1954), 69.
18. See especially Jacques Barzun, *Darwin, Marx, Wagner; Critique of a Heritage* (1941, revised 2nd edition 1958), 10ff., especially 32; and, in defense of Darwin, Richard Hofstadter, *Social Darwinism in American Thought* (revised edition 1955) (hereafter cited as *Social Darwinism*), especially 20ff. Cf. generally, and on Darwin's own discomfort as "godfather" of "social Darwinism," the friendly but discriminating assessment of Gertrude Himmelfarb, *Darwin and the Darwinian Revolution* (1959, reprinted 1962), especially 412–431.
19. Somehow the version attributed to Darwin was thought more tolerant of the efficacy of effort, which thinkers like Lester Ward were concerned to vindicate as against the fatalistic observer's stance associated with Spencer. See Hofstadter, *Social Darwinism,* 139, 233, and the position of Dewey there quoted. And see Henry George's earlier assault on Spencer's fatalism in *Progress and Poverty* (1879), and the discussion in Hofstadter, *Social Darwinism,* 111ff.
20. E.g., Gaston Richard, *L'Origine de l'Idée de Droit* (1892).
21. M. A. Vaccaro, *Les Bases Sociologiques du Droit et de l'Etat* (1898); A. Menger, *Das bürgerliche Recht und die besitzlosen Volksklassen* (1908); and in qualified form much of Weber's and Veblen's thought. See n. 34 below.
22. See, e.g., A. H. Post, *Bausteine für eine allgemeine Rechtswissenschaft auf vergleichende-ethnologischer Basis* (1880–81), and his *Die Grundlagen des Rechts und die Grundzüge seiner Entwickelungsgeschichte* (1884).
23. See Cairns, *Social Sciences,* Ch. 2; H. E. Barnes, "Representative Biological Theories of Society" (1925–26), 17 *Sociological Review* 120–130, 182–194, 294–300; 18 *Sociological Review* 100–105, 231–243, 306–314. And see on Jhering, Stone, *Human Justice,* Ch. 5, §§ 1–7.
24. Samuel Butler, *Erewhon* (1872), *Life and Habit* (1877), and *Evolution, Old & New* (1879). The first part of *Erewhon* to be written was published in article form under the title "Darwin among the Machines" in 1863. See Butler's preface to the revised edition of 1901. And see H. F. Jones, *Charles Darwin and Samuel Butler* (1911); and Barzun's strictures on Darwin's metaphysics in "the bad sense," and his discussion of Butler's and Nietzsche's criticisms, in Barzun, *Darwin, Marx, Wagner,* 101–114.
25. Otto von Gierke's classical work on this matter is *Das deutsche Genossenschaftsrecht* (1868–1913). A section of Vol. 3 is translated with an

introduction by F. W. Maitland as *Political Theories of the Middle Age* (1900). For von Gierke's views on justice not here discussed see W. G. Friedmann, *Legal Theory* (1944, 4th edition 1960), 180–190, especially 189.

26. Lester Ward's writings were primarily in the sociological rather than the juristic stream but it is worth noticing that, like Otto von Gierke, he was trained as a lawyer. Ward's main theses are contained in four works: *Dynamic Sociology* (1883); *The Psychic Forces in Civilization* (1893, 2nd edition 1906); *Applied Sociology* (1906); and *Pure Sociology* (1903, 2nd edition 1925). Cf. H. E. Barnes, "Two Representative Contributions of Sociology to Political Theory: The Doctrines of William Graham Sumner and Lester Frank Ward" (1919), 25 *American Journal of Sociology* 150–170; R. A. Kessler, "Lester F. Ward as Legal Philosopher" (1956), 2 *New York Law Forum* 389.

27. Jean Gabriel de Tarde lived 1843–1904. See his *Les Lois d'Imitation* (1890), translated from 2nd French edition by E. C. Parsons as *The Laws of Imitation* (1903), with a biographical note at iii–vii. Cf. on his work generally Gurvitch, *Sociology of Law*, 103–116; C. K. Allen, *Law in the Making* (6th edition 1958) 97ff. Tarde's theory sprang naturally from his work as chief of the criminal statistics section of the French Ministry of Justice, but he was also during his lifetime a *juge d'instruction*, and a professor of philosophy. His works on criminology and penology (*Criminalité Comparée* (1888); *La Philosophie Pénale* (1890), translated in *Modern Criminal Science Series; Etudes Pénales et Sociales* (1892); *Les Foules et les Sectes Criminelles* (1893)) led him to stress, perhaps unduly, the "contagious" factor in the creation of crime. He developed this idea in relation to law generally in two more general works entitled *Les Transformations du Droit* (1894) and *Les Transformations du Pouvoir* (1899). See Stone, *Social Dimensions*, Ch. 9, §§ 9–10.

28. See Stone, *Social Dimensions*, Ch. 9, § 9, and *passim*.

29. See, e.g., Stone, *Human Justice*, Chs. 2, 10, and *Social Dimensions*, Ch. 12, where it is sought to take account of these.

30. See notably Emile Durkheim, *Le Suicide* (1897). Gustave Le Bon's *Psychologie des Foules* (1895) was a pioneering work in the cognate field of crowd psychology. Later work such as that of Karl Mannheim (see Stone, *Social Dimensions*, Ch. 3, n. 138 and following nn.) and H. D. Lasswell, *Psychopathology and Politics* (1930) and *World Politics and Personal Insecurity* (1935), is largely in this line. On the other hand, Daniel Essertier, *Psychologie et Sociologie* (1927), concluded a comparative study of Le Bon, Durkheim, and Tarde by suggesting as early as 1927 that the simple dualism between individual and collective psychology had been superseded. See Stone, *Social Dimensions*, Ch. 9, §§ 9ff. For other impressive comparative studies see Howard Becker and H. E. Barnes, 1 *Social Thought from Lore to Science* (2 vols., 2nd edition 1952), as to Durkheim, Le Bon, and Spencer; and Talcott Parsons, *The Structure of Social Action* (1937) (hereafter cited as *Social Action*), as to Pareto (Chs. 5, 6), Durkheim (Chs. 8, 11), and Weber (Ch. 17). See especially the critical account in Ch. 8 of Durkheim's *Le Suicide*.

31. The main applications of his theories to law are to be found in Durkheim's *De la Division du Travail Social* (1893), edited and translated by G. Simpson as *On the Division of Labor in Society* (1933). And see more generally G. Aimard, *Durkheim et la Science Economique* (1962); Emile Durkheim, *Sociology and Philosophy* (1953, translated by D. F. Pocock).
32. See Stone, *Social Dimensions*, Chs. 2-3.
33. Cf. Arnold M. Rose, ed., *The Institutions of Advanced Societies* (1958). Spencer had already given a version of evolution as a process by which an indefinite incoherent homogeneity becomes differentiated into a more definite coherent heterogeneity.
34. Max Weber (1864-1920) also did much to import the necessary correctives; see especially his *The Protestant Ethic and the Spirit of Capitalism*, translated by Talcott Parsons (1930), which sought to demonstrate scientifically the substantial (though not determinative) role of ideals and beliefs actually held by groups of men in the determination of social and economic change. Cf. on this thesis Leo Strauss, *Natural Right and History* (1953), 50ff., especially 60-61, n. 22. And see generally Weber's *The Theory of Social and Economic Organization* (translated by A. M. Henderson and Talcott Parsons, 1947); Weber, *General Economic History* (translated by F. H. Knight, 1927); *From Max Weber: Essays in Sociology*, translated and edited by H. H. Gerth and C. W. Mills, 1946; *Max Weber on Law in Economy and Society*, translated by Max Rheinstein, 1954. For the original German see Weber's "Rechtssoziologie," *Wirtschaft und Gesellschaft* (1922), Vol. 21, Pt. 3. For Weber's background see J. P. Mayer, *Max Weber and German Politics* (1944); and for his social theory, Parsons, *Social Action*, Ch. 17. Cf. Barna Horvath, book review of Rheinstein, *Max Weber on Law in Economy and Society* (1956), 5 *American Journal of Comparative Law* 153.
35. (1901) collecting writings over the period 1896-1901. See Chs. 10-27, in which he treats mainly "Public Opinion," "Law," "Belief," "Social Suggestion" (including education and custom), "Social Religion," "Personal Ideals," "Ceremony," "Art," "Personality" (i.e., personality influence), "Social Valuations." And see Stone, *Social Dimensions*, Ch. 14, §§ 1-3, Ch. 15, §§ 1-9.
36. *Ibid.*, 106. Cf. on Karl Renner, Stone, *Social Dimensions*, Ch. 9, § 4, Ch. 10, Ch. 12, § 8, and O. Kahn-Freund's introduction to his English edition of Renner's *Institutions of Private Law and Their Social Functions* (1949), translated by Agnes Schwarzschild.
37. And see Stone, *Human Justice*, Ch. 5, §§ 8-14, and *Social Dimensions*, Ch. 11.
38. See introduction to Ehrlich, *Sociology*.
39. Ehrlich summarized his teachings in a translated article, "Sociology of Law" (1922), 36 *Harvard Law Review* 130. For fuller bibliographical and biographical details see Professor Moll's preface in Ehrlich, *Sociology*, viiff. Ehrlich was professor of Roman law at Czernowitz.
40. Published under the pen name Gnaeus Flavius.
41. Pt. I (1911), 24 *Harvard Law Review* 591; Pt. II (1912), 25 *Harvard Law Review* 140; and Pt. III (1912), 25 *Harvard Law Review* 489;

and his "Need for a Sociological Jurisprudence" (1907), 19 *Green Bag* 107. The work of the Russian Leon Petrazycki on the psychological aspects of law should also be mentioned. See Stone, *Social Dimensions*, Ch. 12, § 4, especially n. 42.

42. And cf. his *Social Control through Law* (1942), 124–125; *Outlines of Lectures on Jurisprudence* (5th edition 1943), 35 (hereafter cited as *Outlines*).

43. See M. G. White, *Social Thought in America, The Revolt against Formalism* (1949) (hereafter cited as *Social Thought*).

44. *Id.,* 11.

45. *Id.,* 12.

46. *Id.,* 7–8.

47. *Id.,* 96–97, 128–146.

48. *Id.,* 25, 76–94.

49. *Id.,* 59–75, 103–106.

50. *Id.,* 20ff., 107ff.

51. *Id.,* 220ff., on the historian J. H. Robinson.

52. Cf. *ibid.*

53. *Id.,* 204ff.

54. *Id.,* 244ff., where he observes of Dwight Waldo, *The Administrative State* (1948), that even "a political technology does require a programme."

55. White, *Social Thought*, 245. See note 59 below. For other pleas that "social science" concerns itself more with "social policy" see G. D. H. Cole, "Sociology and Social Policy" (1957), 8 *British Journal of Sociology* 169, and Gunnar Myrdal's now classical thesis that economics cannot be policy-sterile in *The Political Element in the Development of Economic Theory* (2 vols., translated 1953 from the German edition by Paul Streeten; original Swedish edition 1929), especially Ch. 8, 193, 196. See also E. W. Patterson, *Law in a Scientific Age* (1963), 44ff., and literature there cited; and Stone, *Social Dimensions*, Ch. 4, § 1, and the caveat as to *ad hoc* problem-solving, *id.,* Ch. 1, § 14.

56. Myrdal's work only became available in English after the publication of Stone, *Province*, in 1946. Galbraith's is, of course, of the middle 'fifties. And see Stone, *Social Dimensions*, Ch. 8, 15 *passim.*

57. Some of the literature will be cited later. Not surprisingly, much of it in both the general and the legal areas is collaborative. See, e.g. (by way of random sampling only), Daniel Lerner and H. D. Lasswell, eds., *The Policy Sciences* (1951); Talcott Parsons, E. A. Shils, K. D. Naegele, and J. R. Pitts, eds., *Theories of Society* (2 vols., 1961) (hereafter cited as Parsons *et al., Theories*), a very valuable collection of materials; Gardner Lindzey, ed., *Handbook of Social Psychology* (2 vols., 1954); W. M. Evan, ed., *Law and Sociology, Exploratory Essays* (1962, contributors: W. M. Evan, David Riesman, Talcott Parsons, H. C. Briedemeier, T. A. Cowan, Hans Zeisel, F. L. Strodtbeck, A. W. Blumrosen); F. J. Davis, H. H. Foster *et al., Society and the Law* (1962, a symposium of two lawyers and two sociologists, especially 39–63, 95–310); Howard P. Becker and Alvin Boskoff, eds., *Modern Sociological Theory in Continuity and Change* (1957) (hereafter cited as *Sociological Theory*), an impressive stocktaking, still aiming to main-

tain the refusal "to enter the arena of politics" but with some uneasiness concerning this — see, e.g., Boskoff, introduction, 30–32, and Don Martindale, "Social Disorganization: The Conflict of Normative and Empirical Approaches," at 340ff., especially 366–367); R. K. Merton and Paul F. Lazarsfeld, eds., *Continuities in Social Research* (1950); T. J. Geiger, *Vorstudien zu einer Soziologie des Rechts* (1947).

T. A. Cowan, in Evan, *Law and Sociology*, 94, has indeed suggested that one of the respects in which legal experience may benefit the social scientist is "by making available to him an immense reservoir of *value judgments* on human behavior in the history of law itself and in its present body of empirical rules of decision." And see also *id.*, 98–104; H. Zeisel, "Sociology of Law 1945–55," in the UNESCO trend report on *Sociology in the United States of America* (edited by H. L. Zetterberg, 1956).

58. A most important example of the emerging recognition of limitations on empirical inquiry is of course the economic contribution to the concept of "market power" in anti-trust law, on which see E. S. Mason, "Market Power and Business Conduct" (1956), 46 *American Economic Review* 471, 476ff. The central difficulties are not in lack of facts or their analysis, but of accepted methods and criteria for evaluation, for instance as to the conflicting policies of economic efficiency and curbing of power concentration. See Stone, *Social Dimensions*, Ch. 7, *passim.*

59. See the preliminary study (aided by collaboration among a wide range of social scientists) in P. E. Jacob and J. J. Flink, "Values and Their Function in Decision-Making. Toward an Operational Definition for Use in Public Affairs Research," supplement, May, 1962, to 5 *American Behavioral Scientist*, No. 9. The full program is supported by a Ford Foundation grant. And see other citations, n. 55 above.

60. To the above extent we agree with White, *Social Thought* (1949, epilogue to 1957 edition in 1962 Print 247–280), whose words above quoted are at 258. White is concerned to show that the liberalism of many of Reinhold Niebuhr's political judgments arises from personal qualities of courage and rightmindedness, rather than from the "dark theory of human nature" ("original sin") of his *The Children of Light and the Children of Darkness* (1944). See 257–258. He further thinks that this kind of theory marches with the revival in Walter Lippmann, *Essays in the Public Philosophy* (1955), of "the ancient and obscure theory of essences of natural law," at least in the respect that they are both hostile to political discussion "in the spirit of science" (258). And see *id.*, xii and 274.

It is odd to find related tension with the social sciences in criticism from the Marxist standpoint. A. McIntyre has argued, for example (in E. P. Thompson, ed., *Out of Apathy* (1960), 195, 225–227 (hereafter cited as *Apathy*)), that social scientists like Parsons are caught in the following dilemma: "Either men can discern the laws which govern social development or they cannot. If they can, then the behavior of the scientists themselves is subject to those laws and they are not agents but victims, part of a social process which occurs independently of human mind, feeling or will. If they cannot discern such laws, then they are necessarily helpless, for they have no instruments of change in their hand. So that in any case human agency is bound to be ineffective." For the present purpose we would comment that whatever the force of this dilemma for those who ultimately know all, it has not prevented many interim contributions of the social sciences to the solution of human problems.

61. Insistence on this relevance of empirical knowledge to value-judgment, and not the thesis implied in the title, is the importance of Arnold Brecht's "Myth of Is and Ought" in M. D. Forkosch, *Political Philosophy of Arnold Brecht* (1954), 102–123. And see Stone, *Social Dimensions*, Ch. 12, § 1, especially n. 1; and cf. also Stone, *Human Justice*, Ch. 11, *passim.*

62. Roscoe Pound, "Anachronisms in Law" (1920), 3 *Journal of the American Judicature Society* 142ff., 147.

63. Holmes, "Path of the Law," 261 in his *Collected Legal Papers* (1920), 167, 187.

64. H. E. Yntema, "Legal Science and Reform" (1934), 34 *Columbia Law Review* 207, at 226.

65. Both men had pressed the idea for many years. See for late statements A. T. Vanderbilt, "The Law School in a Changing Society: A Law Center" (1946), 32 *American Bar Association Journal* 525, 528; Roscoe Pound, "A Ministry of Justice: A New Role for the Law School" (1952), 38 *id.* 637–640, 703–705. Cf. Dean E. N. Griswold's address, June 22, 1962, on the dedication of the Ohio Legal Center.

66. Editorial, "The Law Center" (1946), 32 *American Bar Association Journal* 569. Cf. Arthur Nussbaum, "Some Aspects of American 'Legal Realism'" (1959), 12 *Journal of Legal Education* 182, 190–191.

67. And cf. the ten-year project for a Model Penal Code, directed by Professor Herbert Wechsler. A deliberate effort was there made to use the relevant bodies of knowledge from many relevant social disciplines, by a team of lawyers and social scientists, while bearing in mind the special questions involved in *legal* responsibility and punishment.

68. The Berkeley Center has projects for studies of litigants, the role of lawyers in litigation, and courts in their social setting. The Columbia Project has made a number of studies of the legal profession and the speed and *effect* of litigation, e.g., Maurice Rosenberg and M. I. Sovern, "Delay and the Dynamics of Personal Injury Litigation" (1959), 59 *Columbia Law Review* 1115–1170; Maurice Rosenberg and Myra Schubin, "Trial by Lawyer: Compulsory Arbitration of Small Claims in Pennsylvania" (1961), 74 *Harvard Law Review* 448–471; M. A. Franklin, R. H. Chanin, and Irving Mark, "Accidents, Money, and the Law: A Study of the Economics of Personal Injury Litigation" (1961), 61 *Columbia Law Review* 1–39; Maurice Rosenberg and R. H. Chanin, "Auditors in Massachusetts as Antidotes for Delayed Civil Courts" (1961), 110 *University of Pennsylvania Law Review* 27–56.

Besides the New York Institute of Judicial Administration above mentioned, there is also a recently established Institute for Trial Judges at the University of Denver, Colorado. Cf. also the University of Chicago Jury Studies, Stone, *Social Dimensions*, Ch. 1, n. 104a.

69. For a popular account of the United Kingdom position by distinguished

contributors including A. L. Goodhart, Lord Denning, G. L. Williams, see *Law Reform and Law-Making* (1953).

70. The subjects of its reports included the administration of New York courts (1954), children and families in the courts of New York City (1954), the federal loyalty security program (1956); impartial medical testimony (1956); freedom to travel (1958); conflict of interest in the federal service (1956); and a study of automobile accident claims (1962). See, e.g., R. B. Hunting, "Payment for Accident Victims: The Claimant's Eye View" (1961), 33 *New York State Bar Journal* 81-96.

71. The recently established Walter E. Meyer Research Institute of Law (New Haven), devoted to promoting legal research, has sponsored surveys of legal research in procedure (C. Hazard), trusts and trust taxation (T. F. Hogg), anti-trust law, contracts (L. Lipson), criminal law (G. Muller). Its director, R. S. Brown, Jr., sponsored the notable recent symposium on "Frontiers of Legal Research" (see "Legal Research") in an effort to improve interdisciplinary communication.

   With related objectives there was in the 'fifties a National Institute of Mental Health Project for participation of psychiatrists in law school teaching of criminal law, family law, and the law of evidence, at the University of Pennsylvania.

72. A. T. Vanderbilt, *The Idea of a Ministry of Justice Considered and Its Functions Distributed* (1955, 32; also printed as "Address by Chief Justice Vanderbilt" (1955), 78 *Report of New York State Bar Association* 152) (hereafter cited as *Idea of a Ministry of Justice*).

73. For political theory this has now been done by G. A. Almond and J. S. Coleman, *The Politics of the Developing Areas* (1960) (hereafter cited as *Developing Areas*). For a sampling of the special aspects which might need to be taken into account see Stone, *Human Justice*, Ch. 9, §§ 9-13; and Stone, *Social Dimensions*, Ch. 2, §§ 13, 17, and nn. 22, 38; Ch. 3, § 4; and Ch. 4, § 5.

74. This was a main theme of an address by Justice Frankfurter to the Harvard Society of Illinois, April 28, 1955.

75. Cf. some main themes of the Brookings Institution's *Research for Public Policy* (1961), especially of Pendleton Herring and Morton Grodzins. Dean Griswold, address, June 22, 1962, on the dedication of the Ohio Legal Center, endorsed these general points from the standpoint of law school research. Alfred de Grazia and C. L. Ruttenberg ("Innovators in the Study of Legal Process," in "Legal Research," 48-51) have recently tried to survey the personnel available for innovatory work in the law and society area. They list 254 persons from fields embracing in addition to law political science, sociology, philosophy, psychiatry, history, economics, statistics, survey research methods, anthropology, and criminology. This list is presumably of United States personnel, though it includes a few British scholars such as M. Gluckman, S. Toulmin, H. L. A. Hart, and the present writer. They are obviously diffident about its value (see p. 50), and regard disorganization and poor communication between workers as even greater problems than lack of personnel. We would add, as to many of the 254 names listed, that as one swallow does not make a summer, so one tour de force does not make an innovating worker. Moreover, any attempt to designate inno-

vators in the study of legal process on a Gallup poll basis in which the in-novators are also the designators (see de Grazia and Ruttenberg, "In-novators in the Study of Legal Process" in "Legal Research," 48–51) is obviously hazardous. To know what is "innovatory" the designator should be aware of the place of his interests in the stream of learning, jurispru-dential as well as behavioral. A number of the 254 surely did not, yield-ing the result (referred to in one aspect in Stone, *Social Dimensions*, Ch. 1, n. 53a) which Drs. de Grazia and Ruttenberg rightly find strange, that the ten individuals voted "most innovative" apparently never read the works of other innovators, even as avant-garde poets read Shake-speare but not each other (see *id.*, 50, 52).

Program and Movement in the Borderlands of Law and Social Science

1. Roscoe Pound, "Scope and Purpose of Sociological Jurisprudence" (1912), 25 *Harvard Law Review* 489, 513, 516. Professor Pound felt able still to state it as a program in 1943 (*Outlines*, 32–35). And cf. in 1953 Arnold M. Rose, "Problems in the Sociology of Law and Law Enforcement," 6 *Journal of Legal Education* 191. See the appreciations in Julius Stone, "Roscoe Pound and Sociological Jurisprudence" (1965), 78 *Harvard Law Review* 1578–1584; and (more fully) *id.*, "Law and Society in the Age of Roscoe Pound: A Memorial" (1966), *Israel Law Review* (forthcoming).

2. This is probably part (though a misdirected one) of the drive behind the attempt to establish that there is an autonomous "sociology" or "social science" of law, as with Timasheff, Cairns, and Gurvitch. See Stone, *Social Dimensions*, Ch. 1, §§ 7–8.

3. See J. W. Hurst, *The Growth of American Law* (1950), *Law and the Conditions of Freedom in the Nineteenth-Century United States* (1956), *Law and Social Process in United States History* (1960), and *Law and Economic Growth* (1964).

4. As to Parsons see Stone, *Social Dimensions*, Ch. 1, §§ 4–6. And see for S. F. Nadel's final formulation his *The Theory of Social Structure* (1957) (hereafter cited as *Social Structure*).

5. See Nadel, *Social Structure*, 22, discussing T. M. Newcomb in M. Sherif and M. O. Wilson, eds., *Group Relations at the Crossroads* (1953), 36.

6. See Nadel, *Social Structure*, 20ff., 47ff.

7. See Talcott Parsons and E. A. Shils, eds., *Toward a General Theory of Action* (1951), 198ff. (hereafter cited as *Theory of Action*). And see Stone, *Social Dimensions*, Ch. 13, §§ 1ff.

8. Talcott Parsons, *The Social System* (1951), 5, 26.

9. In this very difficult hyphenation Parsons seems to refer to "needs" as these are to be inferred from actual behavior-tendencies of the or-ganism, and manifest in propensities which seek gratification within and often despite the given social setting. It has as its background the conception of personality associated with the work of H. A. Murray. See Murray, W. G. Barrett, Erik Homburger, *et al.*, *Explorations in Personality* (1938, dedicated significantly *inter alia* to Sigmund Freud,

A. N. Whitehead, and Carl C. Jung); M. L. Stein, *The Thematic Apperception Test* (1955, manual for clinical application). And see H. A. Murray and Clyde Kluckhohn, eds., *Personality in Nature, Society, and Culture* (1948, dedicated *inter alia* to Talcott Parsons and other collaborators in founding the Harvard Department of Social Relations). And see the editors' introductory chapter, 5–67, for a general account, especially 14ff. on "need-disposition" as "a vector (directional magnitude) which guides mental, verbal and/or physical processes along a certain course."

10. Parsons, *The Social System*, 11.
11. *Id.*, 27.
12. Cf. B. M. Berger, "On Talcott Parsons" (1962), 34 *Commentary* 507–513, especially 507–509.
13. Parsons, *The Social System*, 38ff. More strictly, perhaps, they are correlative. Moreover, the "sanctions" would strictly appear to be not the role-expectations themselves, but the reaction by the *alter* to the ego's performance *vis-à-vis* these expectations.
14. Parsons, *The Social System*, 42.
15. "Cathectic" orientation refers to the meaning of the object to ego in terms of his "gratification-deprivation balance" (at 7), cathexis being but "the attachment to objects which are gratifying and rejection of those which are noxious": Parsons and Shils, *Theory of Action*, 5. Perhaps "gratification" is the nearest vulgar term. Unfortunately Parsons himself seems to equate it sometimes with "motivational" (e.g., *The Social System*, 12), sometimes with "appreciative" (e.g., *id.*, 13). The former is unfortunate since it overlooks his own point that motivation always comprises cognitive and evaluative as well as (usually) cathectic orientations (*id.*, 12). The latter is unfortunate since it blurs the distinction between cathexis and evaluation. No doubt cathexis may be a main source of evaluation (the Parsonian "cathexis" being then closely approximated by the Thomist "synderesis" (discussed in Stone, *Human Justice*, Ch. 7, § 3), when this is (as it were) de-universalized). Yet Parsons also insists (*The Social System*, 41–42) that the *shared* evaluations in which he is mainly interested "are in general learned or acquired."

As with Pound's *"de facto* interests" somehow molded by the received ideals of the cultural tradition (Stone, *Human Justice*, Ch. 9, §§ 2ff.), so (but more definitely) Parsons's individual evaluations are not, therefore, primarily determined by individual cathexes, but by the learned cultural tradition. Insofar as cathexes operate in this area, they do so rather indirectly through need-dispositions to conformity "as a condition of eliciting the favourable and avoiding the unfavourable reactions of others" (Parsons, *The Social System*, 38), referred to by such psychological notions as "ego-ideal," "self-respect," "adequacy," or "security" (*id.*, 40).
16. *Id.*, 57–58. He has obviously tried hard not to leave out any type of orientation, or distinction among orientations, which at any stage of scientific analysis might ever be of some importance. The general influences of Weber and Freud are clear, though they would be difficult to specify in detail.

17. Parsons, *The Social System*, 24–67, *passim*, with summation at 57–58.

18. Cf. in more mystical form the view of both individual personality and the group, and the interaction of groups within the wider society, as a continuing product of a dynamic process of contradiction and conflict: G. Simmel, *Conflict* (translated by K. H. Wolfe) and *The Web of Group-Affiliations* (translated by R. Bendix), in one volume (1955). E. C. Hughes, in the foreword, 9, characterizes Simmel as "the Freud of the study of society."

    For related problems of interaction in groups see E. Latham, *The Group Basis of Politics* (1952). And for an important recent study of experimental work focused on leadership in small groups, and seeking to pinpoint the limits of translatability of its results to the politico-social process see Sidney Verba, *Small Groups and Political Behavior* (1961), especially 206–244, with bibliography on recent work at 251–270 (hereafter cited as *Small Groups*). And see Joseph Taubman, "Law and Sociology in the Control of Small Groups" (1959), 13 *University of Toronto Law Journal* 23 (hereafter cited as "Law and Sociology").

19. Cf. E. C. Devereux, in Max Black, ed., *The Social Theories of Talcott Parsons* (1961) (hereafter cited as *Talcott Parsons*).

20. See from a socialist standpoint A. McIntyre, in Thompson, *Apathy*, 222–225. Parsons, he thinks, is "submerged by the determinist image of man," studying only those aspects of society mechanistically determinable. And see *id.*, 195, 210–227.

21. Parsons, *The Social System*, 204.

22. See, e.g., *id.*, 36, n. 7, 298. And see (with this) 280ff. for the equilibrium notion as setting limits to deviance from the institutionalized patterns.

23. He presents them rather variably even within *The Social System* itself. Cf., e.g., 46–51, with 58–67 and 101–112; and see Devereux, in Black, *Talcott Parsons*, at 40–44.

24. See Devereux in Black, *Talcott Parsons*, 43. Cf., on Parsons's insistence that these pairs are dichotomies and not continua, Berger, "On Talcott Parsons."

25. See Parsons, *The Social System*, 129–130. Action which in an affectivity-diffuseness relation will tend to produce love, in an affectivity – neutral-diffuseness relation yields esteem; and in an affectivity-specificity relation yields only receptiveness or response.

26. See *id.*, 62ff.

27. *Id.*, 62. The example, however, is not Parsons's.

28. We prefer these terms of Devereux, in Black, *Talcott Parsons*, to the terms "Ascription-Achievement" which Parsons adopts from Ralph Linton, *The Study of Man* (1936), and Linton, "Status and Role," in Parsons *et al.*, *Theories*, 202–208.

29. Cf. Parsons, *The Social System*, 168ff., 178ff. Yet in another sense there is some growth in the importance of status — economic status — as the basis of the regulatory structure of the welfare state. See e.g., on "the new feudalism," Stone, *Social Dimensions*, Ch. 3, § 4, Ch. 4, § 16.

30. See also Devereux, in Black, *Talcott Parsons*, 43, on Parsons's hitherto

only tentative suggestion of a further dichotomy between long-run and short-run valuation.

31. Parsons, *The Social System*, 483.
32. *Id.*, 484ff.
33. Both the importance and the difficulties of the theory as felt by Parsons's fellow sociologists are obvious enough from a perusal of the contributions to Black, *Talcott Parsons*.
34. R. M. Williams, in Black, *Talcott Parsons*, 93; cf. Parsons, *The Social System*, especially 11, on the role of symbolization.
35. Black, *Talcott Parsons*, 279.
36. Berger, "On Talcott Parsons," 510–511, has remarked nevertheless upon the comparative paucity of subsequent research activity attributable to the method afforded by *The Social System*.
37. Parsons, *The Social System*, 25.
38. See, e.g., Stone, *Social Dimensions*, Ch. 3, §§ 8ff.
39. Parsons, *The Social System*, 133ff., 155–156, 171, 187, 207ff., 503–504, 510–512. See also, though not on the above points, Talcott Parsons and R. F. Bales, *Family, Socialization and Interaction Process* (1955). For Parsons's influence in Australian work on the family, see M. S. Brown, in A. P. Elkin, ed., *Marriage and the Family in Australia* (1957), 82–114. And see Stone, *Social Dimensions*, Ch. 6, §§ 7–10.
40. See Parsons, *The Social System*, 221.
41. Sheldon and Eleanor Glueck, *Unraveling Juvenile Delinquency* (1950), 222, 223.
42. I am indebted to my friend Charles Boasson, personally as well as for his account in Boasson, "The Influence of Anxiety and Fear in International Relations" (1958), 4 *Law and Economics* 207, 208 (article also published in Tel Aviv, in Hebrew), for drawing my attention to this notable contemporary example of non-communication among related areas of social science.
43. Much important work has of course pressed independently toward these insights. See the works of J. Bowlby, E. J. Shoben, R. D. Andry, K. S. Beam, S. R. Slavson, and others (including of course the Gluecks). And see Stone, *Social Dimensions*, Ch. 6, § 24.

    Parsons's further insight that early identification with the mother, by boys as well as girls, must produce strain and delinquency-proneness as boys move toward their adult role, e.g., in the occupational system where femininity will hamper, has also given important leads in criminology. See Talcott Parsons, "Certain Primary Sources and Patterns of Aggression in the Social Structure of the Western World" (1947), 10 *Psychiatry* 167–181, A. K. Cohen, *Delinquent Boys: The Culture of the Gang* (1955, English edition with introduction by W. J. H. Sprott, 1956).

    For an important plea for mutual critical evaluation of law and sociology, see Taubman, "Law and Sociology."
44. And even more so, as to blockage between the few behavioral scientists specializing in law itself. Alfred de Grazia *et al.* conclude ("Legal Research," 48–51) from questioning 120 leading "Innovators" in work on law as a behavioral science that they are like the avant-garde poets

mentioned above who read Shakespeare but not each other. It may even be intriguing to ask whether many of them could name a commonly-recognized "Shakespeare." Clearly more mutual advertence, as well as advertence to the now millennial streams of jurisprudential thought, are urgent necessities.

Failure of the sociological and juristic concerns to recognize their mutual relevance is still regrettable even when, because the intellectual approaches are worlds apart, recognition requires a leap of imagination as well. Thus the rarefied and existentialist flavor of Werner Maihofer, "Die Natur der Sache" (1958), 44 *Archiv für Rechts- und Sozial Philosophie* 145-174, and the mutual advertence of Parsons and Maihofer to each other, should not conceal the core of similarity between the Parsonian constructs and Maihofer's insistence on fact relations of life as based on both *entia physica* and *entia moralia* maturing as "cultural fact relations" into "specific conditions of existence" of all beings, grounded on configurations and roles of life, in which entities are "referred" to each other by mutual dependencies manifest centrally in roles and role-expectations. See Stone, *Human Justice*, Ch. 7, § 7, on these positions in relation to theory of justice. And cf. other versions of juristic "nature of facts" speculations also discussed in I. Tammelo, "The Nature of Facts as a Juristic Tópos" in I. Tammelo, A. Blackshield, and E. Campbell, eds., *Australian Studies in Legal Philosophy* (1963), published as special *Beiheft* No. 39 of *Archiv für Rechts- und Sozial Philosophie* (hereafter cited as *Australian Studies*), 237-262, especially 241ff. as to Radbruch's links with Weber, and 245ff. on Maihofer.

45. In Black, *Talcott Parsons*, 90ff. Cf. Berger, "On Talcott Parsons," 511-512; Ralf Dahrendorf, *Class and Conflict in Industrial Society* (1959) (translated, revised, and expanded by the author), 168-170, finds Parsons's emphasis on integration is "untenable and a dangerous onesidedness" (169). Dahrendorf's criticism is accepted to some extent by Black. While neither Parsons nor Dahrendorf accepts fully the "zero-sum" concept of authority (what one has, the other has not) of C. W. Mills, *The Power Elite* (1956), Dahrendorf does accept the fundamental conflict position, concluding that although authority frequently realizes and symbolizes functional integration, in other contexts it may be the representative and exponent of sectional interests only (170). And see Stone, *Social Dimensions*, Ch. 13, n. 60.

46. *Ibid.*

47. See, along Parsonian lines of analysis, S. A. Stouffer, "Analysis of Conflicting Social Norms" (1949), 14 *American Sociological Review* 707, and the citations in Williams, in Black, *Talcott Parsons*, 92n.

48. Jerome Michael and M. J. Adler, *Crime, Law and Social Science* (1933), xii.

49. From this viewpoint, therefore, proposals such as those of Cairns (see Stone, *Social Dimensions*, Ch. 1, § 8) for a pure science seeking the constant relations between the facts of human behavior relevant to social disorder are more appropriately addressed to the social sciences generally. Parsons, *Social Action*, 757-775. Cf. also the view of J. R. Commons (*Legal Foundations of Capitalism* (1924), Ch. 1, especially

9–10, and 82–83) that psychology, economics, jurisprudence, and ethics "look upon the same process from different angles." In any case we should avoid loose language which suggests that *law* itself is or should be a social science, when all that can be meant is that the law ought to be made and administered with intelligent regard to relevant knowledge garnered from the social sciences. Cf. the critique of realist assumptions on this point in Edwin Patterson, *Jurisprudence: Men and Ideas of the Law* (1953), 546ff.; and see Patterson, *Law in a Scientific Age* (1963), 3ff., 25ff., 37ff., 47ff.

50. Parsons, *Social Action,* 757–775.
51. K. N. Llewellyn, "The Normative, the Legal and the Law Jobs: The Problem of Juristic Method" (1940), 49 *Yale Law Journal* 1377 and *passim* (hereafter cited as "Law Jobs"). This observation proceeds from the nature of law noted by Savigny as "the totality of life . . . seen from a specific viewpoint" (quoted in Timasheff, *Sociology of Law,* 343). Cf. "Law is not a particular order of phenomena, as economic, domestic, moral or religious orders are. Law is the manner in which all these phenomena must operate. One could think of courts: yet their activity always regulates these economic, domestic and other situations" (René Worms, *Philosophie des Sciences Sociales* (3 vols., 1903–07), 200–201, quoted in substance in Timasheff, *Sociology of Law,* 343).

It may be argued that a similar comment applies to the subject-matter of psychology or economics. Yet there is a difference in the degree and proportion of distribution. The intrusion of political and legal institutions into the subject-matter of psychology or economics has not, up to the present at least, been a major invasion; nor has it basically changed either the specific method of work or the conclusions – the posited psyche and the demand-supply relation remain. There seems to be no such constant specific focus in the study of law in society. *Pace* Llewellyn, "Law Jobs," 1377n, 1379n, where he says that the "legal" is "the needed keystone to integration of fundamental sociological theory." As to whether "disorder" can, as Cairns suggested, be so regarded, see Stone, *Social Dimensions,* Ch. 1, § 8.

52. See Stone, *Province,* Ch. 1; Stone, *Legal System,* introduction, § 8.
53. See for expansion of these points Stone, *Legal System,* introduction, § 8, and *Social Dimensions,* Ch. 1, §§ 4–6. The present view was widely adopted in 1957 at the third Italian National Congress of Legal Philosophy. See in (1958), 35 *Rivista Internazionale di Filosofia del Diritto,* Guido Fassò, 110–113, at 110; Alessandro Groppali, 126–129; Vincenzo Palazzolo, 189–195; Dino Pasini, 196–206, especially 204. As to the theories of Roberto Ardigò see Giuseppina Nirchio, 170–180; and as to those of Groppali and Luigi Caiani cf. Stone, *Social Dimensions,* Ch. 1, n. 233. See also the valuable analyses in Aurel David, "Metodo Sociologico e Metodo Legislativo" (1957), 34 *Rivista Internazionale di Filosofia del Diritto* 300.
54. We have corresponding reservations as to the theses of Mirra Komarovsky, ed., *Common Frontiers of the Social Sciences* (1957), and of Evan, ed., *Law and Sociology,* 9ff.

Man and Machine in the Search for Justice or Why
Appellate Judges Should Stay Human

1. A selection of the literature to 1963 and an analysis of the issues in relation to lawyers' reasoning will be found in Stone, *Legal System*, Ch. 1, § 10. There are two notable late symposia in *Jurimetrics* (1963, winter), 28 *Law and Contemporary Problems* 1–270 (hereafter cited as *Jurimetrics*), and "Legal Research." The former is a particularly balanced and thoughtful collection containing discussions of the range of "modern logic" (L. E. Allen and Mary Ellen Caldwell, "Modern Logic and Judicial Decision-Making: A Sketch of One View," *Jurimetrics* 213 (hereafter cited as "Modern Logic")); jurimetrics as "the scientific investigation of legal problems" (H. W. Baade, foreword, *Jurimetrics* 1); the mathematical aspects of decision-making (Fred Kort, "Simultaneous Equations and Boolean Algebra in the Analysis of Judicial Decisions," *Jurimetrics* 143 (hereafter cited as "Simultaneous Equations")); methodology with machines in relation to legal research, especially retrieval, and the relation between computer work and symbolic logic (Lee Loevinger, "Jurimetrics: The Methodology of Legal Theory," *Jurimetrics* 5 (hereafter cited as "Jurimetrics: Methodology")); the ability to predict appellate decisions by factorization and statistical methods related to machine potentialities (Glendon A. Schubert, "Judicial Attitudes and Voting Behavior: The 1961 Term of the United States Supreme Court," *Jurimetrics* 100, 108–137 (hereafter cited as "Judicial Attitudes")); fears of the effect of machine limitations on the quality of justice dispensed (J. J. Spengler, "Machine-Made Justice: Some Implications," *Jurimetrics* 36 (hereafter cited as "Machine-Made Justice"); Walter Berns, "Law and Behavioral Science," *Jurimetrics* 185); attempts to dispel such fears (F. R. Dickerson, "Some Jurisprudential Implications of Electronic Data Processing," *Jurimetrics* 53 (hereafter cited as "Jurisprudential Implications")); the use of quantitative methods and probability theory in analyzing judicial materials (S. S. Ulmer, "Quantitative Analysis of Judicial Processes: Some Practical and Theoretical Applications," *Jurimetrics* 164 (hereafter cited as "Quantitative Analysis")).

2. See, e.g., Dickerson, "Jurisprudential Implications," 53, 56–65.

3. See, e.g., *id.*, 65–70.

4. T. L. Becker, "On Science, Political Science, and Law," in "Legal Research," 11–15, especially 14–15.

5. C. F. Stover, "Technology and Law — A Look Ahead" (1963), *Modern Uses of Logic in Law* 1–8.

6. See Berns, "Law and Behavioral Science," 185–212, especially 201–211. And cf. the related polemics within the discipline of political science itself. See Kirkpatrick, "The Impact of the Behavioral Approach on Traditional Political Science" in Austin Ranney, ed., *Essays on the Behavioral Study of Politics* (1962), 1, 28; J. P. Roche, "Political Science and Science Fiction" (1958), 52 *American Political Science Review* 1026ff.

7. See Spengler, "Machine-Made Justice," 36–52. See especially his im-

pressive analysis of the effect of the bias toward machine-handleable concepts on 44–46.

8. See Dickerson, "Jurisprudential Implications," 53, especially 53–55.
9. This undue broadness of confrontation rather dominated the exchanges at the Lake Arrowhead Law and Electronics Conferences, October 1960 and May 1962, under the joint auspices of the U.C.L.A. Committee of Interdisciplinary Studies and the Systems Development Corporation. See generally *id.*, 53ff.
10. T. A. Cowan, "Decision Theory in Law, Science, and Technology" (1963), 140 *Science* 1065, 1072.
11. See Glendon A. Schubert's *Quantitative Analysis of Judicial Behavior* (1959), 320 (hereafter cited as *Judicial Behavior*), insisting that his "scalogram analysis cannot tell us how the court ought to decide future cases," and making the same point as to Fred Kort, "Predicting Supreme Court Decisions Mathematically" (1957), 51 *American Political Science Review* 1–12 (hereafter cited as "Predicting Supreme Court Decisions").
12. See, e.g., S. S. Ulmer, "Scientific Method and Judicial Process" in "Legal Research," 21–22, 25–37. And see Ulmer, "Quantitative Analysis."
13. Schubert, "Judicial Attitudes," 100, 102–103, 105–108.
14. For the present view on this broader matter see Julius Stone, "When Politics Is Harder than Physics" (1963), 32 *American Scholar* 431. Some writers in the area, indeed, are careful to disown any decisive role for such work even in determining the answer to *legal* questions as such. See, e.g., Ulmer, "Quantitative Analysis," 164, 184; Allen and Caldwell, "Modern Logic," 213, 269.
15. Ulmer, "Quantitative Analysis," 164, 184.
16. Allen and Caldwell, "Modern Logic," 213–270. This charming union of esoterics and innocence, however, manifests perhaps too great a degree of indifference to all concerns other than those interesting the authors.
17. Harry Alpert, "Some Observations on the State of Sociology" (1963), 6 *Pacific Sociological Review* 45–48 (Presidential address to the Pacific Sociological Association, April 26, 1963).
18. *Ibid.*
19. See the fuller discussion in Stone, *Social Dimensions*, Ch. 14, §§ 9–13. And on the argumentational aspect see Stone, *Legal System*, Chs. 6–8, especially 8.
20. See, e.g., Ernst Cassirer, *Language and Myth* (translated by Susanne K. Langer, 1946), 37ff.; Joshua Whatmaugh, *Language, A Modern Synthesis* (1956), 68; A. H. Gardiner, *The Theory of Speech and Language* (1932, 2nd edition 1951), 13. Semantic inquiries are seen by some as part of semiotics, being the general theory of signs of all kinds.
21. In its broad sense "semantics" is also used to cover all the three inquiries above. Cf. generally David Rynin, introduction to his edition of A. B. Johnson, *A Treatise on Language* (1959); C. W. Morris, "Foundations of the Theory of Signs" (Vol. 1, No. 2), 1–ii, in Otto Neurath, Rudolf Carnap, and C. W. Morris, eds., *International Encyclopedia of Unified Science* (1938), 6ff. Morris's division is adapted by Rudolf Carnap, *Introduction to Semantics* (1942), 8–11; U. Scar-

pelli, *Il Problema della Definizione e il Concetto di Diritto* (1955), 39. And see generally A. W. Read, "An Account of the Word 'Semantics'" (1948), 4 *Word* 78–97, Stephen Ullmann, *The Principles of Semantics* (1951, 2nd edition 1957), 1–42. It is unnecessary here to canvass many points of continued disagreement among semanticists.

22. The structural linguistic approach differs somewhat, but does not here concern us. See Z. S. Harris, *Methods in Structural Linguistics* (1951), 186ff. If the basic unit of communication is thought of in terms of the minimum expression of *maximum* meaningful content, the work of the electronic engineer suggests that non-linguistic signs may be a more efficient medium, in terms (of course) of information transmission merely. The study of the most economic method of transmitting information (in this sense) is the concern of "information theory," which reflects on the degree of redundancy in linguistic communication.

23. And other terms, none of which, as Ullmann, *Principles of Semantics*, 69, points out, is very satisfactory.

24. We obviously cannot enter here into the sharp debates stirred by logical positivist and related theses on this point.

25. See generally C. K. Ogden and I. A. Richards, *The Meaning of Meaning* (1923), Ch. 1, to be taken however in relation to the later literature cited in Ullmann, *Principles of Semantics*, 65ff. And see Stone, *Legal System*, Ch. 7, Project-note G, especially n. 28.

26. The active mood of this participle is obviously rather inapt; yet it has rather established itself as meaning the thing referred to. See Ullmann, *Principles of Semantics*, 69ff.

27. Attempts to fill this kind of breach, by seeing, e.g., the word "or" as a psychological state of hesitation, need not here be considered.

28. Involved in the broader doctrine of the "area of meaning" "thing-meant" of Gardiner, *Theory of Speech and Language*, 36, on which see also Stone, *Legal System*, Ch. 1, § 6.

29. They are referred to technically as "syncategorematic." See Rynin, in Johnson, *Treatise on Language*, 19.

30. See Gardiner, *Theory of Speech and Language*, § 12; Rynin, in Johnson, *Treatise on Language*, 11. On this view, indeed, even when we usually regard a perceptible thing as the referent, it would be more correct, in view of the purposive nature of speech, to think rather of the "thing meant" as the referent.

31. A term of P. E. Wheelright, *The Burning Fountain* (1954), 61.

32. *Id.*, 35.

33. Cf. Whatmaugh, *Language, A Modern Synthesis*, 176.

34. See Stone, *Legal System*, especially Ch. 6, § 4.

35. See, e.g., A. A. T. Hägerström, *Inquiries into the Nature of Law and Morals* (edited by K. Olivecrona and translated by C. D. Broad, 1953), 17–53.

36. Though having some parallel implications, this difficulty is independent of that of machine handling of semantically vague terms. To this latter problem champions of electronic methods offer two main answers. One is to call on lawyers to shift their emphasis from problems of "interpretation" of documents to adjusting their natural language to a "sterilized" form which will permit extraction of answers by use of machines.

L. E. Allen, "Beyond Document Retrieval toward Information Retrieval" (1963), 47 *Minnesota Law Review* 713–767; Allen, "Automation: Substitute and Supplement in Legal Practice" in "Legal Research," 39–44; and Allen and Caldwell, "Modern Logic," 213–270. And see W. B. Kehl *et al.*, "An Information Retrieval Language for Legal Studies" (1961), 4 *Communications Ass. for Computing Machinery* 380. But on the limited hopes of this in the foreseeable future, and the limited range of lawyers' concerns which it could cover, see Allen and Caldwell, "Modern Logic," 270. The other approach is to stress the adaptability of modern logics for use on semantically vague notions and classes. See especially on the Boolean algebra in this context Dickerson, "Jurisprudential Implications," 53–70, especially 63.

37. See Stone, *Legal System*, Ch. 1, §§ 6–7, Ch. 7, § 17, and Project-note G.
38. *Ibid.*
39. W. K. Wimsatt, Jr., and M. C. Beardsley, *The Verbal Icon* (1954).
40. Or of the theory offered in Stone, *Province*, 200. I owe a special debt to my able student W. K. Dean, B.A. LL.B., for suggesting this correction.
41. An airplane was thus held in 1931 not to be a "motor vehicle" within the Motor Vehicle Theft Act, not because the legislature did not have airplanes in mind, but because people in 1931 did not use and understand "motor vehicle" in that way. Cf. Holmes J. in *McBoye* v. *U.S.* 1931), 282 U.S. 25, 26. Alfred Korzybski, *Science and Sanity* (1933, 2nd edition 1941), among his sounder and more up-to-date proposals, suggested that a date index should be attached to words to help make us aware of these changes. Cf. in recent legal discussion, E. B. Duffy, "Practicing Law and General Semantics" in "Language of Law: A Symposium" (1955), 9 *Western Reserve Law Review* 119; Walter Probert, "Law, Logic and Communication" in "Language of Law: A Symposium" (1955), 9 *Western Reserve Law Review* 129, 135ff. Probert's example – "due process $_{1900}$"; "due process $_{1930}$"; "due process $_{1958}$" – is rather less persuasive than his example "unavoidable accident $_{1500}$"; "unavoidable accident $_{1958}$"; for there is, in any case, a well recognized indeterminacy of "due process" as a standard. And both, of course, are examples in technical legal rather than general usage.

   Of course, on the theory of precedent, judicial determination will bind at a later time; but these very determinations are themselves subject to similar treatment by later generations. See Stone, *Legal System*, Ch. 7, §§ 12–14, especially n. 237, and Ch. 8 *passim*. Of course, too, where the semantic change is so great as to produce absurdity or gross inequity in applying a statute, the principle of semantic change would scarcely forbid the courts to depart (as indeed they do) from the present ordinary meaning sufficiently to reach a sensible result. The words "invaluable" and "valueless" (for example) might exchange their meanings in ordinary usage while a statute using them remains unchanged. "Invaluable" did indeed have the meaning "valueless" in 1640.
42. See, e.g., Stone, *Legal System*, Ch. 6, § 3, as to Portalis and the French Code.
43. Cf. the creativeness *in fact* of the French courts under the Code, and of the Pandectists in adapting the Roman law, Stone, *Legal System*,

Ch. 6, *passim*. And see, on the general point, Probert, "Law, Logic and Communication," 129, 136, especially 135, for an attempt to list the main errors springing from unawareness of the plurisignation of words.

44. This position conforms on the semantic side to the general positions of Cassirer, Whatmaugh, and Ullmann. It also makes sense simultaneously of resort for the study of meaning both to legislative history, and to subsequent administrative practice in general operation, or even other external data which United States courts have admitted in aid of interpretation. See *Federal Power Commission* v. *Panhandle Eastern Pipe Line Company* (1949), 69 *Supreme Court Reporter* 1251. And see the materials collected in H. M. Hart and A. M. Sacks, *Legal Process* (1958), 1287–1406. The interpretation of legislative silence as an indication (or not) of legislative policy favoring the status quo is left in ambiguity by this view, as probably indeed in most cases by any other view available. Cf. Wolfgang Friedmann, "Legal Philosophy and Judicial Lawmaking" (1961), 61 *Columbia Law Review* 820, 838.

45. See Stone, *Legal System*, Ch. 6, § 13, Ch. 7, § 1.

46. So, conversely, and moving from the sublime to the ridiculous, the legislator cannot in the long run tyrannize over the associations which people give to words. Officials formerly termed "sewerage inspectors" were first renamed "sanitary inspectors" to check semantic deterioration. They now (see, e.g., U.K. Sanitary Inspectors (Change of Designation) Act, 1956) have been renamed "Public Health Inspectors." For a while perhaps the rose by another name will not smell so. Yet not for long.

47. See Isabel C. Hungerford, *Poetic Discourse* (1958), 13. T. C. Pollock, *The Nature of Literature, Its Relation to Science, Language and Human Experience* (1942), 56 (hereafter cited as *Nature of Literature*), suggests some difference between "literature" and other writings, in terms of literary as distinct from other "use," but does not really specify what the test of "literary" is. If it is the literary author's supposed ability to control the reader's response to his verbal stimuli, this test is dubious both as to the *ability* of literary, and the inability of non-literary, authors, to do so. Semantically the process of finding the meaning of *Donoghue* v. *Stevenson* (1932), Appeal Cases 562, is no different from the corresponding task as to a novel, or a poem, or some other literary work. On Pollock's more general and valid point see p. 137.

48. Pollock, *Nature of Literature*, 137.

49. *Id.*, 96.

50. We are concerned here of course only with the prescriptive *ratio*. As to the descriptive *ratio* — the explanation, or reasons why in fact the decision that was given was so given — see Julius Stone, "*Ratio* of the *Ratio Decidendi*" (1959), 22 *Modern Law Review* 597, 600–601, and Stone, *Legal System*, Project-note F.

51. See Stone, *Legal System*, Ch. 7, §§ 8ff., Chs. 6–8, *passim*, and *Social Dimensions*, Ch. 14.

52. Stone, *Legal System*, Ch. 7, §§ 12ff.

53. On Richards's later position in his *The Philosophy of Rhetoric* (1936),

see W. K. Wimsatt, Jr., and Cleanth Brooks, *Literary Criticism; A Short History* (1957), 641–644.

54. It is still, e.g., a main theme of C. L. Stevenson, *Ethics and Language* (1945). And see the caveats as to the too wide use of the term "emotive" on 76ff.

55. This, too, is a problem independent of that of machine handling of semantically vague terms, considered in note 36 above.

56. See on the methodology, potentialities, and dangers of machine work *Jurimetrics* in note 1 above.

57. But see as to the capacity of machines and new mathematical techniques to handle semantic vagueness, Dickerson, "Jurisprudential Implications," 52–77, especially 62–65.

58. Mr. R. A. Wilson, Director. See R. A. Wilson, "Computer Retrieval of Case Law" (1962) 16 *Southwestern Law Journal* 409–438. The Pittsburgh director is Mr. J. F. Horty. According to C. R. Tapper, "Lawyers and Machines" (1963), 26 *Modern Law Review* 121, 131–136, there are in all more than 28 projects of various kinds touching law. See especially as to the Pennsylvania work, 133–136. And see the journal *Modern Uses of Logic in Law,* under American Bar Association auspices. And see on the numerous varied current activities *Jurimetrics, passim*; American Bar Association Electric Data Committee, "Legal Research," *passim*; L. E. Allen, R. B. S. Brooks, and Patricia B. James, *Automatic Retrieval of Legal Literature* (1962); E. A. Jones, *Law and Electronics* (1962, 1st Lake Arrowhead Conference Report, 2nd Report forthcoming); *Reports* of three Forums sponsored by the Joint Committee on Continuing Legal Education of the American Law Institute and American Bar Association, held respectively May 23–25, 1961, October 19–21, 1961, and February 1–3, 1962 (for particular legal areas). And see citations in notes 56 and 57 above, 59 below; and the excellent concise survey in R. M. Mersky, "Application of Mechanical and Electronic Devices to Legal Literature" (1963), 11 *Library Trends* 296–305.

59. Figures as in Vanderbilt, *Idea of a Ministry of Justice*; C. R. Tapper, "Lawyers and Machines," 129; J. R. Brown, "Electronic Brains and the Legal Mind: Computing the Data Computer's Collision with Law" (1961), 71 *Yale Law Journal* 239, 251 (hereafter cited as "Electronic Brains"). See especially Judge Brown's thoughtful discussion of other modern complexities, including impacts on the rules of admissibility of evidence, and generally on hitherto empirical and unsystematic common law development, as well as on legal search, 250–254. For literature on the logic side see Brown, "Electronic Brains," 245, and many articles of R. N. Freed, cited 241–242 and *passim*. And see generally H. W. Jones, ed., *Law and Electronics* (1962); F. B. Wiener, "Decision Prediction by Computers: Nonsense Cubed — and Worse" (1962), 48 *American Bar Association Journal* 1023; Nicholas Johnson, "Jurimetrics and the Association of American Law Schools" (1962), 14 *Journal of Legal Education* 385–392; L. Mehl, *Automation in the Legal World* (1958). So far as prediction is concerned we are disposed to agree with Samuel Mermin ("Concerning the Ways of Courts: Reflections Induced by the Wisconsin 'Internal Improvement'

and 'Public Purpose' Cases" (1963), *Wisconsin Law Review* 237) that wherever wisdom and value-judgment enter, as they most usually do, the science of predicting appellate decisions of particular cases (whether by machines or not) is still "pre-Copernican." See Schubert, *Judicial Behavior*, and Schubert, ed., *Judicial Decision-Making* (1963). And cf. generally Dickerson, "Jurisprudential Implications," 53–70. This is not to say that advances should not be sought. See Kort, "Predicting Supreme Court Decisions," 1–12, and "Simultaneous Equations," 143–163; Stuart Nagel, "Weighting Variables in Judicial Prediction" (1960), *Modern Uses of Logic in Law* 93; R. C. Lawlor, "Information Technology and the Law" (1962), 3 *Advances in Computers* 299–352, and "What Computers Can Do: Analysis and Prediction of Judicial Decisions" (1963), 49 *American Bar Association Journal* 337. One basic weakness of the sanguine view is its apparent innocence of the problematics of *stare decisis*. See Lawlor, "What Computers Can Do." And see notes 56 and 57 above.

60. Antecedents in political science concern are usually seen in C. H. Pritchett, *The Roosevelt Court* (1948), and its founding as a movement in Schubert, *Judicial Behavior, Constitutional Politics* (1960), and *Judicial Decision-Making* (a collection of materials). See xiii–xiv of *Judicial Behavior* for other acknowledged antecedents. And see D. J. Danelski, "The Influence of the Chief Justice . . ." in W. F. Murphy and C. H. Pritchett, eds., *Courts, Judges, and Politics* (1961); J. B. Grossman, "Role-Playing and the Analysis of Judicial Behavior: The Case of Mr. Justice Frankfurter" (1962), 11 *Journal of Public Law* 285–309; J. R. Schmidhauser, "Stare Decisis, Dissent, and the Background of Justices of the Supreme Court of the United States" (1962), 14 *University of Toronto Law Journal* 194–212; Martin Shapiro, "Political Jurisprudence" (1964), 52 *Kentucky Law Journal* 294–345.

61. Cf. Schubert, *Judicial Behavior*, 377.

62. On the contest between old-fashioned neo-realist "intuitive" prediction and that of the behavioralist, see Fred Rodell, "For Every Justice, Judicial Deference Is a Sometime Thing" (1962), 50 *Georgetown Law Journal* 700, 707–708; Schubert, "Judicial Attitudes," 100, especially 102–108; and Ulmer, "Quantitative Analysis," 164, 175–176 (as regards Llewellyn and the behavioralist approach). The controversy, though in some respects slightly ridiculous, does nicely point both the common base of the two approaches and the claim of the behavioralists to have achieved by quantitation methods of prediction skill which can be communicated to others.

63. See for the initial systematic statement Schubert, *Judicial Behavior*, 77–172 (bloc analysis), 173–267 (game analysis), 269–376 (scalogram analysis), 377–385 (general account of the methods).

64. See also, for general methodological accounts, G. A. Schubert, "Study of Judicial Decision-Making as an Aspect of Political Behavior" (1958), 52 *American Political Science Review* 1007, and "Judicial Attitudes," 100–142, especially 108ff.; Ulmer, "Quantitative Analysis," 64. For a brief balanced account of computer approaches, linking them with earlier juristic approaches, usually showing due caution as to the limits

of machines in judgment, see Loevinger, "Jurimetrics: Methodology," 5, especially 30–35.

The main distinction among machine methods is between the more obvious analysis by subject-matter on the one hand, and analysis by reference to language units on the other. The latter, working as it were in smaller units, has more potentialities of range and refinement, but it involves far more elaborate and complex systeming. For the main alternative approaches on the language basis see Loevinger, especially 10–13 (Pittsburgh "key words in combination" project), 13–16 (the Western Reserve "semantic coded abstract" method), 17–19 (the "association factor" method), 19–22 (probabilistic indexing of key words to discover the more important latent classes of relevant matters). Cf., covering similar ground, W. B. Eldridge and Sally F. Dennis, "The Computer as a Tool for Legal Research," *Jurimetrics*, 71, 78–99. And see Loevinger, 16–17, and Eldridge and Dennis, 89–90, for an approach directly via subject-matter in the Oklahoma State "points of law" approach. On indexing and abstracting problems generally, see Loevinger, 27–30; on the need for use of a variety of searching strategies, Eldridge and Dennis, 94–99. And see the pilot project report in J. S. Melton and R. C. Bensing, "Searching Legal Literature Electronically" (1960), 45 *Minnesota Law Review* 229–258.

For a critique of current bloc analysis methods, as used, e.g., by Schubert, see J. D. Sprague, "Voting Patterns on the U.S. Supreme Court Cases in Federalism 1889–1959" (thesis, Stanford University, using data from 2,839 cases collected by Dr. R. A. Horn, of which 831 cases from 30 courts were "divided" cases; Sprague's MS thesis, 1964, at University Microfilms, Ann Arbor, Michigan (hereafter cited as "Voting Patterns")), Chs. ii, iii; and 190–194 for a denial that the Supreme Court's divided decisions from 1889 to 1930 manifest polarization, and for the ambiguity of the data after 1930. And see note 65 below.

65. For recent claims as to predictive accuracy in Supreme Court civil rights and economic policy cases, see Schubert, "Judicial Attitudes," 100; Ulmer, "Quantitative Analysis," 164.

Sprague, "Voting Patterns," 95–100, finds, however, that in 831 divided decisions between 1889 and 1930 no case classification for unidimensionality of attitudes by means of Guttman scaling reached the .90 level of reproducibility for even half of the 30 courts involved. Schubert's more favorable assessment is (Sprague thinks) based on three kinds of methodological vice: (1) the effect of conventions adopted to deal with changes of personnel or non-participation by particular justices; (2) the tendency to work in short time-spans of one court, variations obviously tending to be less in shorter spans; (3) the *non sequitur* that accuracy of prediction warrants the method used to predict. There can be "quite accurate predictions that the sun will rise tomorrow . . . on the basis of quite erroneous theories." Sprague draws important attention to Guttman's own recognition that the unidimensionality indicated by a high coefficient of reproducibility may be spurious, for instance because the cases basing the prediction may all be of non-scale types.

66. We here develop somewhat further a point of R. S. Brown, Jr., "Legal Research: The Resource Base and Traditional Approaches" in "Legal Research," 3, 5–6. For other computer functions relevant but not special to legal concerns, see Loevinger, "Jurimetrics: Methodology," 30–31.

67. See for caveats on this matter notes 64 and 65 above.

68. Cf. also the mooted use of the new techniques to test the reliability of jury verdicts, even in criminal cases. See the interesting preliminary analysis in this area of Ulmer, "Quantitative Analysis," 176–183. And cf. the well-known Chicago jury studies, Zeisel, "Social Research on the Law," in Evan, ed., *Law and Sociology*, 124; Loevinger, "Jurimetrics: Methodology," 32–33. And see Rita M. James, "Status and Competence of Jurors" (1959), 64 *American Journal of Sociology* 563–570 (empirical observation at simulated trials).

69. Where it is held (as, e.g., in Wisconsin) that in case of such doubt the lower court must make up its own mind regardless of the probabilities of future appellate holdings, the lower court must of course make a judgment similar to that of the appellate "judgment of justice" discussed in succeeding paragraphs.

70. See S. S. Nagel, "A Conceptual Scheme of the Judicial Process," in "Legal Research," 7–10 (hereafter cited as "Conceptual Scheme").

71. It is not to deny the value of the schematization for further research to ask social scientists to be more aware that the substance of what is involved has usually been well discussed, and often for a long time, in the juristic literature. See, e.g., recently, W. V. Schaeffer, *Precedent and Policy* (1956, Ernst Freund Lecture, University of Chicago), R. J. Traynor, *"La Rude Vita, La Dolce Giustizia"*; or Hard Cases Can Make Good Law" (1962), 29 *University of Chicago Law Review* 223–236; R. A. Leflar, "Some Observations Concerning Judicial Opinions" (1961), 61 *Columbia Law Review* 810, all by perceptive judges writing within the sociological juristic tradition without the aid of behavioralist novelties.

72. If (as we do not believe) Nagel's scheme were designed to help the man in the judgment seat, it would be entrancing to speculate how at their "height" Justices Black and Frankfurter would (operating with it) have assessed the effect of the reaction of each of them on the other as it ought to influence a judgment he was engaged in writing. It would be even more entrancing to speculate how they *should* have assessed it.

73. We have in mind, e.g., an interesting project of D. J. Danelski which the present writer was able to peruse at the Center for Advanced Study in the Behavioral Sciences in 1963.

74. This difficulty might perhaps be sidestepped by translating respect for the law into preference for the value of "certainty" or the like. *Sed quaere?*

75. Nagel, "Conceptual Scheme," 7–10, seems to accept the need for this wider canvas.

76. We may adapt to this point Sprague's perceptive comment ("Voting Patterns") that "the issue is not whether attitudes determine judicial behaviour but whether judicial behaviour is determined by a small number of discoverable unidimensional attitudes," discoverable (we

would add) in behavior which has been manifest in the past *before the present moment and context* of judgment.

See, e.g., Berns's claim ("Law and Behavioral Science," 184–212, especially 187–195) that G. A. Schubert shifts between explicit denial that his work proves that Supreme Court Justices play for power, and the adoption implicitly of that very model as a basis of analysis and prediction. Cf. Spengler's thesis in "Machine-Made Justice," 36, 41–43, 50–52, that a bias is involved in the very trimming and selection of data for handling by computer and related techniques. And cf. generally F. M. Fisher, "Mathematical Analysis of Supreme Court Decisions: The Use and Abuse of Quantitative Methods" (1958), 52 *American Political Science Review* 321–338; and the reply by Fred Kort, "Reply to Fisher's Mathematical Analysis of Supreme Court Decisions" (1958), 52 *American Political Science Review* 339–348; P. C. Lawlor, "Information Technology and the Law" (1962), 3 *Advances in Computers* 328.

77. Italics supplied. Takeo Hayakawa, "Legal Science and Judicial Behavior — With Particular Reference to Civil Liberties in the Japanese Supreme Court" (1962), 2 *Kobe University Law Review; International Edition* 1, 22–23. For a projection (not in terms of advocacy) of machine development which would retrieve not only precedent legal data, but also data as to current public value-positions, and other factual social data (à la Brandeis brief), and be programed to process these variables according to assigned values and yield a "judicious" decision in their light, see Becker, "On Science, Political Science, and Law," 11 at 13–14.

78. Baade, foreword, *Jurimetrics*, 3–4. Cf. the even more generalized attack in Berns, "Law and Behavioral Science," 185–212.

79. Stone, *Province*, Ch. vii, now much developed in *Legal System*, Chs. 6–8, and *Social Dimensions*, Ch. 14.

80. See Stone, *Legal System*, Ch. 8.

81. See, however, for a pessimistic view of the difficulties involved in attempting to program more selectively, i.e., to "forget and ignore" creatively, T. A. Cowan, "Decision Theory in Law, Science and Technology" (1963), 17 *Rutgers Law Review* 449–530. There is a current joint project of the American Bar Foundation and the I.B.M. Corporation on automatic organization and retrieval of legal literature designed to build a degree of learning into the machine operations. It proceeds on progressive discrimination by the machine at various levels between words, according to frequency of occurrence in contexts indicating degrees of closeness of relevance to legal discourse and to particular subjects of legal discourse. It is proposed to be based upon 5,800 cases, reports of which have been transferred to magnetic tape. See the account by Eldridge and Dennis, "The Computer as a Tool of Legal Research," 78, 95–99, and on the Western Reserve project Jessica S. Melton, "The 'Semantic Coded Abstract' Approach" (1962), *Modern Uses of Logic in Law* 48.

82. Loevinger, "Jurimetrics: Methodology," 5, at 31. Cf. P. J. Stone, R. F. Bales, J. Z. Namenwirth, and D. M. Ogilvie, "The General Inquirer:

A Computer System for Content Analysis and Retrieval Based on the Sentence as a Unit of Information" (1962), 7 *Behavioral Science* 484.

83. Indeed Schubert, *Judicial Behavior*, 320, observes approvingly of Kort's "Predicting Supreme Court Decisions," 1–12, that it serves only to "construct a model to measure the empirical deviation of the Court from the way it should have behaved under the principle of *stare decisis*." (Kort himself is certainly well aware that the consistency thus sought, e.g., as to what facts are "material" in each case, presupposes a value judgment.) See Stone, *Legal System*, Ch. 7, §§ 12ff. So R. C. Lawlor's work, which perhaps comes nearest to a concentration on prediction as such, seeks to make it possible by developing a "new theory of precedent" to use computers to develop "personal quotations" for individual judges even in cases involving "new sub-sets of acts." See his "What Computers Can Do"; "Foundations of Logical Legal Decision Making" (1963), *Modern Uses of Logic in Law* 98; and an unpublished paper "Analysis and Prediction . . . by . . . Computers" (kindly furnished by Mr. Lawlor, who is a practicing lawyer).

84. For the important caveats on the claims that behavioralist methods have proved their predictive power, see Sprague, "Voting Patterns," and, above, note 64, paragraph 3, and note 65.

85. Baade, foreword, *Jurimetrics*, 3. And see Becker, "On Science, Political Science, and Law," 12–13, and the thesis of C. L. Black, *The People and the Court* (1960). For other lines of current criticism see also Wallace Mendelson, "Neo-Behavioral Approach to the Judicial Process: A Critique" (1963), 57 *American Political Science Review* 593–603; and Shapiro, "Political Jurisprudence."

86. Cf. on the limits of guidance from machines to appellate judges in the judgment of justice from an appellate judge's standpoint P. J. Traynor, "No Magic Words Could Do It Justice" (1961), 49 *California Law Review* 625–626.

87. See for a development of this point Stone, *Social Dimensions*, Ch. 14, § § 12–13.

88. Neglect of existing juristic learning leads frequently to adventures in the reinvention of the wheel. For example, we find political scientists in 1964 offering the poles of activism/restraint as a "dominant-variable" for behavioral analysis of judicial decisions. See H. J. Spaeth, "Judicial Power as a Variable Motivating Supreme Court Behavior" (1962), 6 *Midwest Journal of Political Science* 54–82, and then cf. earlier, in a mass of *juristic* variations on this theme, Sir Frederick Pollock, "Judicial Caution and Valour" (1929), 45 *Law Quarterly Review* 293.

Index

INDEX

INDEX

Jurisprudence, sociological, *see* Sociological jurisprudence
Justice: early concepts of, 4–5; theories of, 5, 6, 9, 18–19, 21, 75–76, 83; role of judge in administration of, 7, 53, 57, 75–76, 78–79, 82–85; approaches to study of, 18, 54, 55, 79; law centers for study of, 23; problem of delays in, 28; use of computers in administration of, 51, 52, 71, 78–79, 82; as an abstraction, 58, 63; quality of depends on humans, 82–83, 84–85. *See also* Behavioralists; Computers; Decision-making

Kampf um die Rechtswissenschaft, Der (Kantorowicz), 13
Kantorowicz, Hermann, 3, 13

Labor Relations Board, 68
Law, sociology of, *see* Sociological jurisprudence
Law and Society Center, at Berkeley, 23
Law center: role of, 22–23, 68
Law Center of University of Pittsburgh, 68
Legal realists: traceable to Holmes, 15; compared with behavioralists, 69–71
Legal research: in social sciences, 6, 22, 71–72; institutions for, 21–22, 23, 68; problems of, 24; use of computers for, 67–68, 69, 71–72, 83. *See also* Behavioralists; Computers
Legislation: institutions for research on, 21–22; role of language in interpretation of, 57–59, 60–61; literal interpretation of, 58–59; British interpretation of, 60; French interpretation of, 61
Lettres Persanes (Montesquieu), 9
Llewellyn, Karl, 6, 81
London, 23

Maine, Sir Henry, 14: founder of English historical school, 4, 8
Malinowski, Bronislaw Kasper: on law in primitive societies, 33
Mansfield, Earl of (William Murray), 68

Marx, Karl, 12, 16
Marxism: legal theories of, 7, 13; interpretation of history of, 15, 16, 17
Meaning of Meaning, The (Ogden and Richards), 67
Ministries of Justice: movement to establish, 21
Montesquieu (Charles de Secondat): impact on later thinkers, 9
Moses, 8
Murray, William (Earl of Mansfield), 68
Myrdal, Gunnar, 18

Nadel, S. F.: role theory in work of, 29–30
Natural law, 74: challenged by Montesquieu, 9; reacted to by Savigny, 14
Neo-Realist sociological jurisprudence, 6
New York City, 23
New York University, 23

Ogden, C. K., 67
Ombudsman (parliamentary commissioner), 22
Origin of Species, The (Darwin), 10, 11
Original sin, doctrine of, 19

Pandectists, 14, 26, 61
Pareto, Vilfredo, 12, 35
Parsons, Talcott, 19, 20, 27, 44: role theory in work of, 29, 31, 34–35, 35–37, 39–40, 41–43; criticism of, 36, 37, 41, 43–44, 45–46; on family relations, 41–43, 43–44; classification of social sciences, 47
Pennsylvania, 68
Pennsylvania, University of, 19
Philosophy, discipline of, 15, 16, 22
Pittsburgh, University of, 68
Plato, 9
Political science: knowledge of useful to jurists, 6, 22; in Parsons' classification, 47; effect of techniques of on law, 50, 70, 73; use of computers in, 77
Pollock, Sir Frederick, 81

INDEX

Ulmer, S. S., 55

United Kingdom, 25: legal agencies in, 22; legal research in, 23; interpretation of legislation in, 60; number of legal cases in, 68–69

United States: legal agencies in, 21–22; statutes in, 21, 68; legal research in, 22–23, 71–72; beginnings of sociological jurisprudence in, 26; number of legal cases in, 68

United States Patent Office: use of computers in, 68

Utilitarianism: of Jhering, 14; influence on role theory, 41

Vanderbilt, Arthur T., 68: advocates legal research in social sciences, 22, 23

Veblen, Thorstein: influence on merging of social sciences, 15

Volksgeist, 8

Ward, Lester, 11, 12

Weber, Max, 12, 35

White, Morton, 15: on anti-formalists, 14, 15–16; quoted, 19

Williams, R. M., 45

Wisconsin, 9

World War I, 26

Yntema, Hessel: calls for institutes of legal research, 22